ROBUST CONTROL SYSTEM NETWORKS

HOW TO ACHIEVE RELIABLE CONTROL AFTER STUXNET

ROBUST CONTROL SYSTEM NETWORKS

HOW TO ACHIEVE RELIABLE CONTROL AFTER STUXNET

RALPH LANGNER

MOMENTUM PRESS

MOMENTUM PRESS, LLC, NEW YORK

Published by Momentum Press®, LLC
222 East 46th Street, New York, NY 10017
www.momentumpress.net

ISBN-13: 978-1-60650-300-3 (hard back, case bound)
ISBN-10: 1-60650-300-6 (hard back, case bound)
ISBN-13: 978-1-60650-302-7 (e-book)
ISBN-10: 1-60650-302-2 (e-book)
http://www.momentumpress.net/10.5643/978606503027

Cover design by Jonathan Pennell
Interior design by Derryfield Publishing, LLC

10 9 8 7 6 5 4 3 2 1

Contents

Preface

The Stuxnet computer virus, originally discovered in July 2010, qualified as a turning point for control system security. While the malware did not cause destructive damage outside its designated target, it hit the Western world like the *Sputnik* shock. The sophistication and aggressiveness of this computer virus was at a level that few people had anticipated. It simply popped up without warning, after 10 years of silence following the first malicious amateur-style cyber attack on wastewater control systems in Australia. Compared to office IT malware as we know it, this would be like going from 1980s-style password guessing to botnets in one step. It was, indeed, shocking. Instead of a learning curve for both the attackers and the defenders that the general development and trend of malware had been experiencing in the IT world, there was one big leap. Even if they had wanted to, operators of potential targets in critical infrastructure and in the private sector were not able to perform a similar leap in defense and protection. Despite years, reaching back to the turn of the millennium, of efforts and investments in control system security, governmental programs and organizations, industry standards, workgroups, conferences, risk assessments, and mitigation projects, the industrialized nations continue to face a significant threat from post-Stuxnet malware for which they are by no means prepared.

While some are quick to say that asset owners and control system vendors simply do not care enough about IT security, I believe this cannot be the complete answer. Doing more risk assessments, installing more firewalls, updating antivirus signatures more frequently, applying more security patches more often, are simply *more* of what has been done already, of what brought us to where we were when Stuxnet was discovered, and where we continue to be: unprepared and vulnerable. So, rather than doing more of the same, it might be a better idea to look for alternatives: alternative concepts and methods that do not necessarily replace the existing school of thought, which largely borrows from IT security, but that complement it. A paradigm shift seems to be mandated by existing methodology inadequacies. While it has often been said that Stuxnet was a wakeup call, it barely interrupted the long and deep sleep of stakeholders in the automation space. After only a few weeks, many of them fell back asleep again, helped by the self-induced illusion that something like Stuxnet couldn't happen to them. The sober insight from this is that the concept of risk has been abused more often to argue risk away rather than being used as motivation and guidance to arrive at more reliable and secure systems.

Over recent years in my position as a consultant for control system security, I have learned that IT security paradigms do not integrate well with engineering methodology and culture. Based on these observations, this book is an attempt to lay out the theoretical and methodological foundation for what I and many other practitioners had already been doing mostly intuitively. Basically, it is a short introduction to the control theory of complex automation and control networks, along with a best-practice guide on how to make such systems more robust. I had realized some time ago that while attempting to make industrial automation and control system (IACS) installations more secure, I was actually making fragile systems more robust. I also realized that IACS installations can benefit from this process even in the absence of recognizable cyber security threats.

One crucial reason for little overall success of IT security efforts on the plant floor appears to be the fact that engineers tend to approach problems differently. They are usually not eager to contemplate hypothetical threats and cyber attackers, and often they wouldn't have the time even if they wanted to. My experience is that control system security as we know it has little appeal to the type of engineer who is vitally needed to improve the security posture of cyber systems on the plant floor. This must change. Therefore this book addresses the subject from the perspective, and in the language, of a control systems engineer. As the reader will note, the terms *availability, confidentiality,* and *integrity* of information are virtually absent from this book, and so is the concept of risk (except in Chapter 1). The general approach taken is to treat cyber just like any other item on the plant floor— to treat data communication links like conveyor belts or pipes, databases like tanks, and data processors like reactors. It is not claimed that this approach is any better than what has been done based on IT security principles and practices; it is just claimed that viewing the growing number of problems in control system security from a different perspective can't hurt. Chapter 2 explains that insufficient control system reliability can and will be caused by unstructured growth of system complexity—even without the presence of adversaries such as hackers, crackers, or malware.

The knowledgeable reader will recognize that the approach taken blends several well-established concepts and methods from control theory, systems theory, cybernetics, and quality engineering. For example, one could very well read this text as quality engineering applied to IACS design and operation, remembering the words of quality pioneer William Edwards Deming: "If I had to reduce my message to management to just a few words, I'd say it all has to do with reducing variation" (Deming, 1982).

The target audience for this book includes plant planners, operators, and maintenance engineers at asset owners who are responsible for planning and maintaining plants with a high degree of automation. Intimate familiarity with the architecture and details of control systems is assumed. What the reader will *not* see in this book are elaborations on Bode, H infinity, and Matlab (anyone interested in learning about controller robustness on a micro-level is referred to Marcel Sidi's *Design of Robust Control Systems* (Sidi, 2001). Instead, topics such as Taguchi (Taguchi et al., 2005), standard operating procedures (SOPs), and UML should be expected. For readers who are especially interested in Stuxnet, there's good news and bad news. Bad news first: Little detail on Stuxnet will be given. Even worse, most examples of real-world incidents in the book are about nonintentional threats, and for a good reason. While very few installations have experienced a sophisticated, directed attack on their control systems, many operators and maintenance engineers have had experiences similar to those described in this book—everyday hiccups that signal that something is at odds with a control system network. Anyone interested in cyberwar may find the examples outright boring. Good news: Following the advice given will help much to prepare for becoming immune not just to those trivial hiccups, but even to the next generation of Stuxnet-inspired malware.

Acknowledgments

The author accepts full responsibility for the thoughts and methods detailed in this book but wants to thank Eric Byres, Eric Cosman, Stefan Lüders, Bryan Singer, and Joe Weiss for contributing valuable comments. Credit also goes to Walt Boyes, who motivated the author to expand the original dense academic-style text to what is (hopefully) more readable and more interesting for the general engineering population.

The Figure 3.1 photos of Sammy, the office clerk, are courtesy of Guido Menebröcker.

All cited examples of cybertrips or noteworthy observations from the plant floor with no identification of the affected facility are taken from the author's personal experience.

About the Author

Ralph Langner received his academic education and degree in psychology, where he focused his research, some of it published, on human information processing as modeled by cybernetics and artificial intelligence. After graduating, he started a software and consulting company in the industrial IT sector. Over the last decade, this same company, Langner Communications, has become a leading European consultancy for control system security. The author received worldwide recognition for his analysis of the Stuxnet malware, which became infamous not only as the most complex malware in history but also as the first malware to target industrial control systems. Information on Langner Communications can be found at www.langner.com/en.

Chapter 1

Introduction: The Three Faces of Risk

Are you, or is the organization you are working for, at risk with respect to the reliability of the control systems you may be responsible for? The answer to this question depends on your concept of risk: To a large extent, recognizing risk is a deliberate choice, and basically a question of accepted responsibility. In general, there are three major schools of thought, coming from different traditions, which teach overlapping concepts of risk that in some way are familiar to everybody who thinks about risk even in layman's terms. The differences are mostly in the fine print of methodology, yet they may lead to vastly differing results. Depending on which risk model you choose, you may argue the risk of cyber-related problems in a complex IACS network away, or you may end up discovering a whole lot of new problems.

1.1 The Insurance Model of Risk: Risk as Statistical Probability and Projected Amount of Loss

A good deal of our intuitive everyday understanding of risk comes from the insurance industry, where *risk* is defined as the cost of consequences multiplied by the mathematical probability that such consequences will materialize for a certain individual—as part of a specific population (such as heavy smokers, mountain climbers, or racecar drivers)—and for a specified time frame. With an empirical database, the frequency of specific unfavorable conditions (such as lung cancer) can be established for a specific population over a defined period of time, and from there, statistical probabilities can be computed, given that the sample is statistically representative of the respective population. A big advantage of this model is that it does not require insight into any causes that might trigger the consequence. So, for example, in medicine, where this model has provided the basic rationale for epidemiology for decades, it is used to determine the probability of falling victim to a specific disease even if the exact cause of the disease is unknown.

The risk equation,

$$\text{Risk} = \text{consequence} \times \text{probability}$$

has for long been a guideline for most discussions about risk. However, many people ignore that in the insurance model of risk, the equation is actually thought of as algebraic and computational, not just figuratively.

There are several problems with this model of risk when applied to control system security. First, the number of control system cyber security incidents on the record is slim. Actually, there are only a handfull. Even if a high estimated number of unknown cases is taken into account, what we see and project is still a very small number of cases. Let's assume there have been 1,000 control system cyber incidents of significant size over the last 10 years. Statistically, this translates to an average of 100 incidents per year, for the global population of installations equipped with control systems, which sums to several million. Thus, the statistical probability of a single installation experiencing a significant cyber incident is minimal.

However, we also have to take into account the cost of the consequence. If the cost of the consequence is huge, even highly improbable events may pose a significant risk. (The terrorist attack on New York City on September 11, 2001, is a good example.) So let's look at the cost of selected major cyber incidents on the record.

> *First, there is the well-documented malicious sewage dump that occurred 2000 in Australia (Weiss, 2010). While subject-matter experts who examined the case say that the attacker caused $3.5 million (U.S.) in damage, he was sentenced in a court of law to pay the equivalent of $7,000 indemnity. Which number is correct: What was the "real" cost of the damage?*
>
> *After the 2003 East Coast power blackout, the federal commission that investigated this cyber-related incident stated that*

it cost is "between $4 and $10 billion." That's a quite impressive difference of $6 billion.

What is the cost of the damage resulting from Stuxnet? Certainly that depends on whether we take into account only the cost of Stuxnet's dedicated victim to recover from the attack and the largely political cost of the outcome, or whether we also include collateral damage in the rest of the world. In any case, it is not possible to attach a hard dollar amount to the damage done.

No matter which of the major cases in history we're looking at, quantifying the cost of consequences is barely possible. And this is for cyber incidents on the record, not for hypothetical incidents that might happen in the future. For the latter, the cost of consequences is almost impossible to calculate. The more so is the probability.

Practical implications: Why should you care about control system security? The answer is, "You shouldn't." In statistical terms, the negative consequences of control system security incidents on the record is so small that it doesn't justify any investment in countermeasures. And after all, no matter how much you invest in countermeasures, you will never be able to achieve 100% security, so no matter what you do, you will still be insecure.

1.2   The Logical Model of Risk: Risk as Cause and Consequence

ISA-99, the broadest and most mature industry effort to elaborate and standardize control system security concepts, defines *risk* as "an expectation of loss expressed as the probability that a particular threat will exploit a particular vulnerability with a particular consequence" (ISA, 2007). In this school of thought, risk occurs as a singular event in time as the result of a threat exploiting a vulnerability, which then leads to a security incident. In short notation,

Threat and vulnerability → incident

In other words, the threat is a *root cause*, and a vulnerability is a *necessary condition*. When both are present, an incident results as a *logical consequence*.

As the ISA definition illustrates, this concept of risk is based on *expectations,* or predictions about future events, which must in some way make assumptions about the behavior of potential attackers (Langner and Singer,

2008). Unfortunately, whenever human behavior is predicted, such as when predicting the actions of potential attackers, predictions may ultimately result in wild speculations that are driven largely by interest. Security researchers and vendors of security products (who benefit from perceived high threat levels) tend to exaggerate threats, whereas asset owners (who benefit from perceived low threat levels) tend to deny threats. Even where there is evidence of threats and related risks, one may choose simply not to trust the underlying prediction. The majority of smokers know very well about the risk that their behavior will result in health problems, but still choose to think that they will only happen to others. After all, there are heavy smokers who live to age 90 and beyond, and there's little reason why I can't. This seems to be one major reason why most efforts to increase industrial cyber security have not succeeded to any reasonable extent over the last decade: Decision makers interpret the chances of not being hit by a cyber security incident in their favor, so there seems to be no reason to invest in countermeasures. There is also a methodological barrier: *The prediction of externalities is not an engineering discipline.*

The aim of security efforts is the prevention of damage caused by attacks that might happen in the future. On the other hand, they might not happen at all. Risk is uncertain. If it were not, it would be fate. There is an epistemological problem with this part of the risk concept, as pointed by Nassim Taleb in *The Black Swan* (Taleb, 2007). If risk mitigation is successful, incidents don't materialize, but there may be no evidence that they *would have happened* in the absence of countermeasures. This might lead decision makers to believe that investments in countermeasures were a waste of money. Many IT security people have already experienced discussions with executives based on this misconception. The worst (yet very common) misunderstanding within this school of thought is to assume that the absence of incidents on the record implies the absence of threat. Nobody learned that lesson more expensively than the American people. Before 9/11, it could be argued that the threat of terrorists flying passenger airplanes into buildings was nonexistent, because it had never been attempted. The deeper epistemological problem is that, from an empirical point of view, the well-protected facility that did not encounter security incidents because of the effectiveness of countermeasures and the ill-protected facility that did not encounter incidents just by plain luck are hardly distinguishable. A record with no cyber incidents does not imply that security countermeasures were successful—it might simply be due to the fact that no attacks were attempted, for whatever reason.

Practical implications: Why should you care about control system security? The answer, again, is, "You shouldn't." After all, you're not a high-priority military target, and a nation state would see no benefit in attacking you with a cyber weapon in a Stuxnet-like scenario. And you can't do anything against insider threats, right? The sobering bottom line is that the logical model of risk has more often been abused to argue risk away rather than to plan and implement mitigation strategies. In consequence, asset owners following this school of thought will only start taking control system security seriously after having experienced a major cyber security incident, which is the convincing argument for being at risk. (A subgroup may even argue that, after having just experienced an incident, there is no need to mitigate risk because the probability of being hit again will be even lower than before, just like the chance of being hit twice by lightning.) Since the goal of security efforts is to *prevent* incidents, practitioners working in environments where this philosophy is exercised may experience high levels of frustration.

1.3   The Financial Model of Risk: Risk as Volatility

Yet another model of risk focuses not so much on cause and consequence, as manifested in singular events, as on *volatility*, which is very similar (if not identical) to variability. This concept is often used in the financial markets. For example, an investment broker may point out that a specific investment opportunity is more "risky" than others, simply because it is more volatile. That means, the return value of such investments underlies unpredictable variation within an estimated range, which may span, for example, from 10 times profit to complete loss of the investment. The return value of more "safe," or "risk-free" investment opportunities, on the other hand, is relatively fixed—that is, variation is very small. Examples include bonds issued by highly rated nation states or blue-chip corporations. Depending on the preference of the investor, a risky investment might sound like a good idea, because volatility also offers the chance for a big profit, whereas a "risk-free" investment never offers such a chance. In finance, volatility, or risk, isn't bad per se. In industrial automation, it is. Figure 1-1 illustrates risk as the span between potential upper and lower limits of a specific variable as it develops over time. Risk spreads where the variable's development is associated with uncertainty.

Volatility, and thus risk in this conceptual framework, is due to *uncontrollable variation of factors with determining influence on performance*. For example, the performance of equity stock of a start-up company depends on factors such as the development of markets, products, the success of marketing campaigns, etc., which cannot be predicted with any reasonable certainty. All such factors are virtually absent in "safe" investments, such as state bonds. It is pretty much predictable that when the time comes, a nation state such as the United States, Germany, or Japan will pay exactly the negotiated amount of money (they certainly won't pay more). Little uncontrollable variation can be found here. It has been argued that one reason for the 2008 financial crisis was that uncontrollable variation was *hidden* in complex derivates such as collaterized loan obligations, thereby hiding risk (Shiller, 2008).

A system shows "volatile" behavior if it is not fully controlled. The behavior of such a system is dependent on *uncontrolled* factors, therefore it cannot be predicted accurately. Reducing these uncontrolled factors (and not all of them may be uncontrollable) will reduce undesired variation of output behavior, or volatility, or risk.

Practical implications: Why should you care about control system security? Because you realize that you're losing control. That's something that you, as a control system engineer or a stakeholder in a highly automated technical process, care about. You realize that with growing cyber complexity of your installation, you're losing reliability and maintainability. That is something that you, as an engineer, care about.

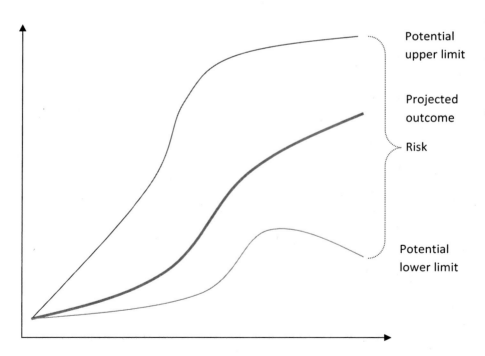

Potential upper limit

Projected outcome

Risk

Potential lower limit

Figure 1-1 In finance, only the portion of risk (= deviation from projected outcome) that is below the bold line is "bad"; the upper deviation is "good." In control, deviation from target values is never "good."

1.4   From Risk to Fragility and from Security to Robustness

For those who prefer to associate efforts to enhance the reliability and security of control systems to the concept of risk, the financial model matches best with the approach taken in this book. It is unrelated to the prediction of externalities, and to the computation of statistical probability and extent of loss. In other words, it is unrelated to efforts that have proven very difficult, unfruitful, and frustrating for engineers.

The average engineer will perhaps have as little affiliation with loan obligations as with insurance death tables or formal logic. Taking this into account, this book transforms the financial model of risk to cybernetics, which is much easier than one might think. Instead of *high risk* and *low risk,* the terms *fragility* and *robustness* will be used. Since mechanical and electrical aspects of automated processes and their control won't be discussed in this book, these concepts will be limited to *cyber fragility* and *cyber robustness*. The reader who reads through the whole book will recognize that when working with these two basic concepts, it is actually no longer necessary to use the term *risk* at all. The benefit of talking less about risk (and more about robustness, reliability, and maintainability) is that decision makers will argue less that the whole problem might be only hypothetical. Little guesswork and crystal ball looking is required to determine the fragility or robustness of a control system installation. As will be shown, while risk and security are hypothetical, fragility and robustness are factual.

Chapter 2

The Problem of Cyber Fragility in Industrial Automation and Control

On March 7, 2008, unit 2 of the Hatch nuclear power plant in Baxley, Georgia, was automatically shut down by its safety systems. As it turned out, the reason for shutdown was a software update which was performed by an authorized administrator on a computer system that resided in the plant's business network. Further investigation revealed that the reboot which was required to activate the update caused a period of communication silence which was interpreted by the safety system, interacting with the server in the business network, as a drop in water reservoirs used for cooling. While the safety system's response was conformant with specification when viewed in isolation, the interaction of events was not anticipated, undesired, and costly.

The Hatch incident highlights a problem that is prominent in many automated facilities: Modern control systems and automation equipment, with their increasingly more complex integration and interrelations, are no longer fully understood—not even in nuclear power plants. Seemingly trivial everyday procedures and events, compliant with policy and in accordance with best practices, carried out by authorized and trained staff, lead to unexpected and undesired consequences that may result in process disruption, quality impairment, and significant loss. Subsequent analysis then reveals that such consequences were bound to happen, and could have been prevented easily. They were simply outside the scope of design and operational procedures. In some cases, it may also be determined that a slightly different combination of everyday procedures would have led to even more undesired, potentially catastrophic consequences.

What this illustrates is *fragility* of complex industrial automation and control systems: Cyber-related events well inside the spectrum of "normal" behavior and environmental conditions cause control systems to misbehave and fail. Fragility is not about catastrophic events such as an electromagnetic pulse (EMP) attack; it's about unsuspicious everyday events that may even have been planned and executed with the best intent, and in accordance with policy. While some of these events happen by chance, others may be forecast to the exact minute, such as the Y2K problem in certain software programs. An IACS installation may have proven to be the most solid implementation that one could wish for and have performed flawlessly for many years, yet fail instantly due to some unsuspicious little variation of the bits and bytes in its environment. In such situations, it then turns out (usually in the aftermath) that the cyber limits of process control were more restricted than anticipated—and documented.

Incidents similar to Hatch occur about every other day in highly automated industrial environments, across industries. This book is about understanding why they happen, and what can be done to prevent them. It will be argued that efforts to prevent such everyday glitches will also significantly improve the cyber security posture of a given installation, making it immune to even the most sophisticated cyber threats. To put it another way, as long as a control system installation is prone to glitches like the Hatch incident, it makes little sense even to try to protect against sophisticated malicious threats.

2.1   Cyber Fragility Defined

Cyber fragility is the deficient ability of an automated process to withstand variations of "normal" conditions for data processing, data storage, and data transmission during the process's lifetime, even when variation is within the limits of typical operating environment characteristics, and analysis shows that such variation could and should have been anticipated. A fragile process or system "breaks" when it is subject to minimal structural modification or variation of environmental conditions. Breakage may manifest not only in structure but also in function and adaptability, and may cause undesired consequences in many different areas, such as production stoppage, quality impairments, or even safety incidents.

A fragile system is like a house of cards (see Figure 2-1). Whoever built the house was well aware that even slight and absolutely "normal" variation in the environment (a window that was opened, a cat that walked by, the presence of a little child who enjoys destroying such structures) may cause the artwork to tumble. Collapse must also be expected during a meticulous attempt to replace a card, i.e., variation of structure. Even the building process itself requires a bit of luck, and more than one attempt may be necessary to arrive at the final construction. The originator usually is proud of having finished the work.

> *After having explained the structure of a complex automation function that pairs product data with product container IDs through interaction between different layers of automation systems spanning from production to logistics execution, the system designer, an experienced control systems engineer, says to the author with a slight undertone of pride, "If you know what's going on behind the scenes, you cannot help wondering that it really works." Absolutely, but there is no reason to be proud of it.*

Cyber fragility reduces the reliability and maintainability of industrial automation and control systems. For the purpose of this discussion,

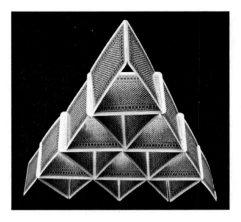

Figure 2-1   A fragile structure. It will hardly withstand even slight environmental changes which are perfectly typical for its environment (in this case, the author's living room). Nevertheless, it may make its creator proud of having built it.

reliability is defined as the ability of a system to perform specified function-ality on demand. *Maintainability* is defined as the ability to regain specified functionality of a system in the shortest amount of time possible, both for unplanned maintenance events (troubleshooting) and planned maintenance events (reconfiguration due to requirement change). Rather than using the term *cyber incident* for operational failures, *cyber trip* is preferred, as inci-dents in general tend to be associated with hazards, and cyber incidents in particular with the actual or potential violation of the confidentiality, integ-rity, or availability (a.k.a. CIA) of information. ISA-99 defines the term *inci-dent* as follows: "Event that is not part of the expected operation of a system or service that causes or may cause an interruption to, or a reduction in the quality of the service provided by the system." The negative effects of cyber fragility, however, may be caused by completely ordinary circumstances that cannot be considered hazards at all, as in the example of the Hatch nuclear facility, and are not necessarily related to the CIA of information, as will be detailed throughout this book. Cyber fragility trips are characterized by the following attributes:

- Causes are noncatastrophic; rather, they are typical conditions and occurrences of the given environment which could have reasonably been expected to occur (some are even planned).
- Often the causes of cyber trips are discovered only months later.
- If human behavior is involved, it may have been fully compliant with policy and standard operating procedure (if such exist).
- Operators and maintenance engineers are caught by surprise by what seems to be a miracle, even though. . . .
- Cyber fragility trips are deterministic, can be explained easily in the aftermath, and could have been prevented easily.

Effects of Cyber Fragility on Maintainability

Cyber fragility manifest not only in cyber trips but also in reduced main-tainability. As with any flexible technology, using such technology to create complex systems requires superimposition of structure, otherwise flexibility will be lost when the structure is exploited heavily on the micro level.

This lesson had been learned expensively in software development, where growing unstructured program code resulted in software programs that could no longer be maintained, and ultimately had to be rewritten from scratch. With the deliberate use of global variables, type casts, memory pointers, and program jumps ("gotos"), all of which were invented and used in the name of flexibility, the maintainability of such code became inversely correlated with program size. This experience heralded the demise of the C programming language, which formerly used to be praised for the freedom it gave to the programmer. However, with growing complexity, flexibility degrades along with maintainability. Such insight led in the 1970s to structured programming (the Pascal programming language by Niklaus Wirth) and to object-oriented programming in the 1980s (the C++ programming language by Bjarne Stroustrup, followed by the Java programming language by James Gosling). When viewed closely, both approaches limit the freedom of the software developer in order to maintain flexibility in the face of growing complexity and adaptability requirements. Perhaps the most expensive lesson learned about the cost of unstructured code was the Y2K problem, when thousands of software programs had to be rewritten from scratch simply because a date format needed to be adjusted.

With growing system complexity, flexibility needs structure, otherwise it devolves to complete system lockup—which is identical to complete inflexibility. One could view the robustness strategies presented later as a similar approach to *structure* IACS design and procedures *in order to maintain flexibility*. There has already be more than one situation where IACS installations appeared to be locked up beyond adaptability by "worst practices" such as direct PLC memory addressing via the network, making deliberate use of TCP connections with self-invented ports and protocols, or creating a pool of shared directories where nobody is able to keep track of required communications any longer.

A *design lockup* can be imagined as a house of cards for which one of the lower cards needs to be replaced—which is simply not possible without rebuilding the whole structure from scratch. Another drawback of flexibility in engineering tends to be overlooked easily. For systems with static behavior and long lifecycle, flexibility is rarely needed. With respect to cyber, flexibility is often abused to overcome shortcomings in the planning and design phases. The easy adaptability of cyber parameters (such as TCP port numbers, IP addresses, or operating system versions) to given needs may lead to improvised, untested, undocumented, and heterogeneous solutions.

Summing up, cyber fragility manifests in trips, in maintenance efforts that are much higher than necessary and anticipated, and in system design lockups. *Systems become fragile when they grow in complexity without developing higher-level structure.* In the next section, it will be shown that this is exactly what has characterized mainstream development in industrial automation and control over the last decades.

Table 2-1   Evolution of Automation Technology

Timeline	Implementation of Control Logic	Technology/ Products/ Architectures	Enabling Technologies
1950s	Hardwired (actual wires)	Electromechanical controls	Relays
1960s	Hardwired (PCBs)	Electronic controls	Transistors
Flexibility Leap			
1970s	Programmable	Programmable logic controllers	Microcontrollers
1980s	Distributed	Standalone DCS (decentralized I/O, but usually standalone server); PLCs + SCADA applications	Mid-size and small computers; Fieldbus
Complexity Leap			
1990s	Integrated	Networked (LAN) architectures with Windows PCs and office applications	Windows PCs, local area networks, TCP/IP
2000s	Collaborative	Multichannel traffic to and from peripherals; multisite; Internet-based remote access, automated quality control, condition monitoring, Manufacturing Execution Systems (MES), efficiency applications (OEE)	Middleware (OPC, MQS), Internet/VPN, Web technologies (HTTP, XML, Java), WLAN, real-time Ethernet

2.2   The Evolution of Complexity in Industrial Automation and Control

Contrary to what contemporary common language use suggests, the term *cyber* does not refer to IT in general; actually, it predates information technology and computers. The term cyber derives from *cybernetics*, introduced in 1947 by Norbert Wiener, laying the ground for what later became automation technology. The term *cybernetics* itself was derived from the Greek noun *kybernetes*, or steersman. The subject of cybernetics was defined by Wiener as "control and communication in the animal and the machine" (Wiener, 1965). (The difference between *cyber* and *information technology* is discussed in Appendix C.) Table 2-1 gives a brief rundown of the cyber evolution in industrial automation and control.

Two major milestones stand out in this evolutionary process, which enabled highly dynamic and efficient systems. The first was the development toward *dynamic control logic,* providing for flexibility. It started in the 1970s with the advent of programmable logic controllers. With simple old-style controllers, control logic was static. The only way to manipulate output was to change an input signal or adjust a setpoint. After a closed-loop controller was installed, one could walk away, come back a year later, and expect the system to do exactly the same thing as at the time of commissioning. This is no longer the case for modern IACS, where control logic isn't hardwired, but programmable. Certainly, the actual control logic that is loaded on the controller has as much influence on output manipulation as input values and setpoints.

The second milestone was the push toward *integration and network connectivity* with third-party systems. It started at the end of the 1980s. What once was a small and simple self-contained system (controller) then became a complex distributed system that interlocked with complex material logistics and business processes. Hardwired control logic within one small black box evolved into digital commands and responses transmitted via standard network infrastructure, including WAN links. All components of a modern control system installation come with "open" data and command interfaces. State-of-the-art process control integrates logistics, scheduling, quality, process optimization, and business logic. In systems theory, this is called *emergence*. Emergence is a property of complex systems in general. Integration with IT and business applications, the growth of cyber space in industrial automation and control, has been the enabling factor for high-level "superfunctions" to emerge. It is not just that some process value can be displayed in a Web browser in real time, it is that groups of systems and logistic chains can be controlled and monitored by automated software processes that may extend to business processes. The behavior of an IACS cannot be understood by looking at it on the component level. While at the controller level behavior might still look like closed-loop architectures opening and closing valves or similar, the same installation might be able not only to produce a car, but also produce a car in the shortest amount of time possible, with near-zero defects, near-zero material buffering, built-to-order, and accepting product configuration changes up to the last hour.

In a modern IACS environment, the behavior of controlled variables is no longer determined just by input values and static control logic. Instead, controlled variables are also sensitive to and dependent on many other factors that may be difficult to predict (remember the financial model of risk), such as the following:

- Setpoint manipulations via the network, originating from multiple anonymous sources
- Changes of control logic via the network
- Adding, removing, or reconfiguring control nodes at runtime
- Changes of the execution environment (patching, updating, or virtualizing the operating system, for example)
- Changes of controller state (run/stop) via digital commands
- Changes of the configuration of supportive infrastructure, e.g., DHCP address changes, DNS server tables, Active Directory server configurations, etc.
- Alterations of data processing, transport, and storage characteristics

All of these make for highly flexible installations, but also for installations that place much higher burdens on reliability and maintainability. It should not be a surprise that the 20-year period from 1990 through 2010 was characterized not only by nuclear power plant outages caused by planned maintenance (Hatch), but also by the first actual cyber warfare attack involving a cyber weapon that caused physical damage (Stuxnet). Nevertheless, the driving factor for this development is not an increased presence of cyber threats, it is growing system complexity, or, to be more specific, growing entropy.

2.3   Entropy and IACS Networks

Entropy is the variation potential of a complex system, or its potential chaos. Entropy is very high in large IACS networks because of the many degrees of freedom that characterize such systems, because of the dynamic behavior, and because of the extremely high order that IACS must maintain over a long period of time—usually more than 10 years. Put very briefly for the purpose of this book, *entropy* is the inverse of the statistical probability that a system arrives at its target state randomly. A coin has a lower entropy than a die, because the probability of the coin landing on its face when thrown is 0.5, while the probability of the die showing a specific number is 0.17. The probability that a complex control system arrives at a particular desired state just randomly is astronomically low, and gets even lower when considering that this state must be maintained over a long period of time. According to the second law of thermodynamics, the more entropy, the more effort is required to maintain order.

> *In a conventional fieldbus installation (Foundation Fieldbus, Interbus, Profibus, etc.), there is a very limited number of accessible systems (let's say 255), and the possible transmissions and commands are even more limited. Usually, only one system (the bus master) has the freedom to send data spontaneously, and there are very limited actions that can be provoked in slave systems. In an industrial Ethernet installation, on the other hand, the number of accessible systems may be several thousand, and the number of accessing systems is also not limited to one; accessing systems may even be remote. The Ethernet and IP address space is much bigger than with fieldbus systems, allowing for more potential of error (think of subnet masks, for example). On top of that, there is a choice of protocols (TCP, UDP), and on top of that, there is a choice of port numbers. Port numbers alone allow for more than 65,000 possibilities of error per transport. Further, there are application-layer protocols which allow for further parameters (and, thus, for error). Interpretation of parameters may depend on context (the state the system is in) and on other communications that take place simultaneously.*

In a boxing match, the colors of the opponents' trunks hardly matters. Each fighter can pick any color he wants. Unless they are twins, both fighters can even pick the same color without risking the audience confusing the parties. The situation is different in a football, soccer, or basketball game. If the players of each team chose their uniform colors individually, they may still be able to recognize the other members of their team, but the audience probably won't be able to. To take the comparison even further, let's imagine a land battle in the eighteenth or nineteenth century, which absolutely required both sides to wear very colorful and very distinct uniforms. Applied to factory automation, one could think of a modern automobile factory, where it is possible (and required to maintain competitiveness) to produce every car in sequence with a different color, which the customer might even be able to change until several hours before actual production. If, due to some problem with pipes, pumps, valves, controllers, etc., the ability to arbitrarily choose any color for every car is lost, production will likely come to a halt. In an old-style automobile factory with a less integrated (and less customer-friendly) production process, consequences would be much less severe, as it would not have been a big problem to produce a shift's load of cars of the same color. And in the days of Henry Ford, the problem was nonexistent because of zero entropy—as Ford famously noted, the customer could have any color as long as it was black.

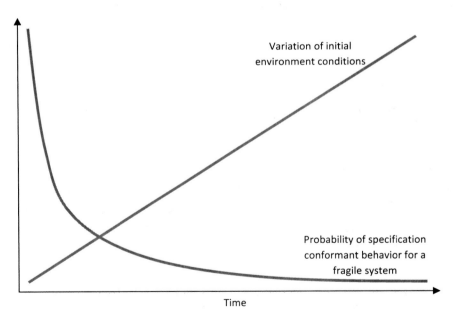

Figure 2-2   While random variation of the environment may increment linearly over time, the reliability of a fragile system decreases exponentially.

The Entropy Process

Entropy is related not only to variation range, but also to time. Very simplified, the concept of entropy implies that every system is moving toward a state of maximum disorder. This is a process that takes place gradually over time. Not all variables change all at once, which would be an ordered change. Therefore, the amount of disorder increases, and so does the probability that some variation occurs which causes a given system to degrade in functionality, and ultimately to fail. Let's go back, for example, to the house of cards. There is very little probability that the house will collapse within the first millisecond after it is finished. There is higher probability that it will collapse within the first minute, the first hour, and so on. It is very unlikely that it will still be standing the next day, or the next week. As can be seen in Figure 2-2, the statistical probability that a fragile system will function (its reliability) is disproportional to time: It decreases *exponentially.*

A typical IACS installation has a lifetime of approximately 15 years. All through the lifecycle, it is required to provide exactly accurate commands and parameters, every day, every hour, perhaps even every second or millisecond. Not less concerning is the probability of change during the installation's lifetime. During an average IACS life span, many variations in operating environment can and must be expected, from equipment failure during operating system updates to nonavailability (in terms of procurement) of what is suddenly going to be considered obsolete technology. While it is hardly imaginable that at some point in time a 24-V power supply will no longer be available, most seasoned engineers have experienced more than once that during the lifetime of an IACS installation, a specific OS version, DBMS version, application software version, or product (HMI, SCADA, CAQ, OEE, etc.), IT hardware product, network technology, etc., becomes obsolete and is simply no longer available for purchase. Examples include 10-Mbps network gear, the Windows NT operating system, or the DCOM technology that forms the technological base for OPC. Even if such obsolete technology or product versions were available, chances are that many times, the newer version would be installed, introducing potential version conflicts. Therefore, simply because of long lifetime, IACS must either be able to tolerate more variation than office IT systems, or it must be shielded against such variation. The same is true on a micro level. While the average office application runs several hours per day (with the exception of server processes), IACS software applications may run for weeks or months, continuously exchanging data via the network.

With the introduction of Windows XP service pack 2, OPC installations did no longer run properly, as Microsoft had introduced a new set of access control parameters called "security limits." This was not a new version of the operating system, but a service pack. What one can learn is that, with respect to control systems, every service pack and security patch should be treated as a new operating system version.

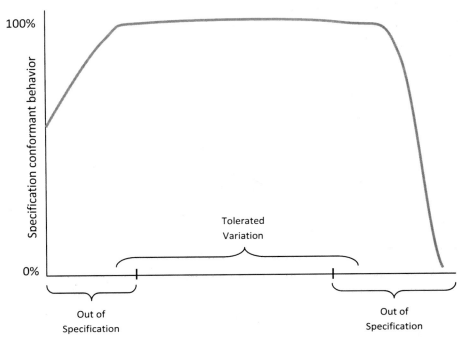

Figure 2-3 An ideal (robust) system. It performs specification conformant even beyond specification limits and tolerates cyber variation of a typical environment.

2.4 Cyber Contingency

It is theoretically possible to define and experimentally measure the cyber limits in which a given IACS performs as desired, as shown in Figure 2-3. In practice, this may be a problem because of combinatorial explosion, as will be pointed out later. The variation of cyber variables beyond such limits is where control degrades. Such limits may be thought of as cyber tripwires that may be reached in contingency situations, and then cause process control to trip. In analogy to statistical process control, they may also be called control limits, as shown in Figure 2-4.

When thinking about the performance of a given technical system with respect to variation of operational parameters, what one *expects to see* will look more or less like Figure 2-3. The system characterized there performs to specification all over the specification limits, and even slightly beyond. Such behavior applies to the electrical and mechanical characteristics of many systems in a typical industrial automation environment. However, it is not typical for cyber. Figure 2-4 illustrates a more realistic example in which one can see that performance degrades even for typical changes in the cyber environment. Variability as measured on the horizontal axis may refer to different cyber parameters, including network latency, antivirus product versions, broadcast packets, free memory space, etc. Unfortunately, not all cyber parameters that affect the behavior of a control system or automation product—and therefore the controlled process—are tested, specified, and documented for many contemporary products and "bespoke" solutions. For example, while one vendor may explicitly prohibit the use of VLAN, OS security patches, or antivirus software for its DCS or SCADA product, many others may just not make any statement at all about how this may affect their products, leaving the question completely open to the end user, who tends to believe that if there is no mention in the system's documentation, there is no problem (whereas the vendor's legal department sees it just the other way around).

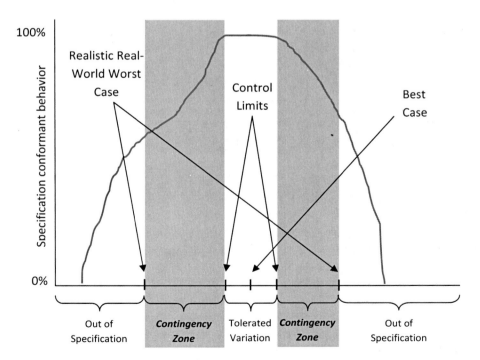

Figure 2-4   A real-world system. It behaves specification conformant only within limits that are more narrow than variation for a typical environment. Control limits are usually not documented, sometimes not even known to the vendor.

Contingency is unfavorable variation that is part of the typical environment of the system under consideration. Contingency conditions are not catastrophic, and most such conditions are not extreme outliers in the statistical sense. The term *contingency* as used here refers to variation in the potential to impair the reliability of a cyber installation. Contingencies should not be confused with emergencies; they fall well within the "normal" bandwidth of variation for the typical environment that the system or process under consideration is designed to support. Just because cyber contingency is related to parameters which are not necessarily identified as critical, such parameters may tend to be overlooked by system designers and operators. However, the more complex a system gets, the more severe may be the consequences of such seemingly nonessential parameters. Design decisions and operational procedures that do not take contingency into account are fragile. They rely on best-case assumptions, which is particularly dangerous in situations and environments where such assumptions are not even documented and the respective environmental cyber characteristics are not monitored.

> *Commercial airplanes are required by law to carry an additional fuel load known as "contingency fuel" so that pilots can cope with imponderables that might prolong calculated flight time (ATC rerouting, stronger headwind than forecast, etc.). It is not known in advance whether such contingencies will actually emerge during flight, but neither is it known that they won't—a classic example of uncertainty. The known fact is that an aircraft will discontinue to fly when fuel is depleted. So on one side there is an uncertainty (with respect to environmental conditions), and on the other side there is a certain outcome (in terms of system behavior, namely, the inability to keep the airplane flying with no fuel left).*

What one can learn from this aviation policy is that even if certain circumstances are not predictable, this is no reason that they should (or can) be ignored. The preferred strategy for guaranteeing mission success (landing an airplane safely, or exercising full control of an automated production process) is to know operational limitations and provide for the capability to tolerate variation. In general, for any IACS there are cyber conditions under which functionality is unimpaired, and cyber conditions under which functionality will be impaired, distorted, or interrupted—contingency areas. The virtual lines that separate the best-case area from contingency areas can be imagined as virtual tripwires for digital process control. As long as cyber parameters are within the virtual boundaries, everything goes according to plan, giving the illusion of full process control. However, once a boundary is reached, process control trips. If this happens, fragility becomes manifest. Many times, it could have been identified much earlier in a lab environment.

The reliability of any system or process in a given environment can only be determined if the conditions are specified at which the system or process under consideration fails. This is common practice for electrical and environmental parameters (such as humidity and dust), but it is usually not documented for cyber conditions. Sometimes, it is not even tested. A fragile system tends to break in the face of contingencies, whereas a robust system will continue to perform even beyond specification limits. To stress the contingency fuel example from aviation, not only do many control system operators not know about potential adverse outside effects that are beyond their control (comparable to unfavorable winds, air traffic congestion, etc.), they don't know the status of factors they could control. Figuratively speaking, they don't know how much fuel they have in their tank, or when this fuel will be depleted. In cyber terms, such fuel may be something like network latency, system accessibility by anonymous agents, or lacking resilience against normal but interfering network traffic.

Cyber Contingency Theory: The Inverse Pyramid of Contingency Layers

The ISO/OSI model of layered communication is well known. A similar model can be established for cyber contingency of digital control systems. Just imagine the ISO/OSI model for a second, in which all starts at the bottom of the physical transmission layer. If communication at this layer is corrupted, it makes little sense to worry about potential problems on the upper layers. Now let's abstract from data transmission, because cyber is also related to data storage and data processing. In Figure 2-5, the different layers of cyber contingency are visualized as an inverse pyramid, because with every layer (or degree of freedom), potential problems accumulate, if not multiply.

The various layers indicate different ways for a specific command, instruction or message to vary and thus cause problems for an IACS and its controlled physical processes:

> **Binary layer:** The binary layer is about whether a specific service, data set, function, etc., is available or not. It is about a simple on/off, yes/no decision. Data that is missing—e.g., due to hardware failure—results in functional failures and cascade effects most of the time. A practical

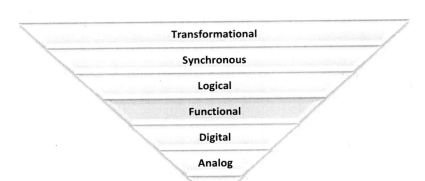

Figure 2-5　The inverse pyramid of cyber contingency. Contingency cumulates with every variation layer, or degree of freedom.

problem is that plant planners, operators, and maintenance engineers often are not aware of all subsystems that are required to function for full functionality of a given system.

Analog layer: Even with everything being digital in a contemporary control system, there are some significant performance and reliability characteristics that are analog. The analog layer is about variability in terms of the speed and/or volume at which data is processed, transported, or stored. Many IACS components are sensitive to data that is processed, transported or stored too slowly or too fast, which may be due to changes in network throughput and latency, processing speed, or memory space. So conditions where too much, too few, too slow or too fast may result in a reduction of IACS reliability and performance are situated on this layer.

Digital layer: Even if bits in the analog layer are within limits, there may be coding problems at the digital layer. This layer is about malformed, corrupted, or otherwise inappropriately coded data that may cause problems when being processed. This is not limited to corrupted data but includes well-formed data that may cause the system to crash due to insufficient resilience, so digital contingency is not only about syntactically well-formed or malformed data and network packets.

Functional layer: The functional layer (highlighted in Figure 2-5) is what most process engineers traditionally conceive as their biggest area of concern. It is about the content of parameters (process variables, configuration values, ladder logic commands, etc.), about legitimate commands that simply put the process or its result out of bounds, such as incorrect speeds, temperatures, timings, or incorrect amounts of recipe ingredients.

Logical layer: The logical layer involves data that is well formed but inappropriate for the system's given state or context. An example is manipulation of the control logic of production controllers.

Synchronous layer: The synchronous layer is about whether data, which may be well formed and legitimate, is transported, executed, or stored at the right time, where the criterion is external—the state or condition of a separate system or subsystem. This includes commands sent to drives for axis synchronization, reading and processing sensor values for quality data at the exact time of sampling, or proper sequencing of logistic chains. Contingency in the synchronous layer may lead to lost productivity due to unnecessary yields (logistics), severely corrupt quality data (perhaps followed by scrapping acceptable products), or material damage (as in the case of inaccurate axis synchronization).

Transformational layer: The transformational layer involves variation that is completely "outside the box," such as a change in requirements. Such a change in requirements may be beyond a system's capabilities and thus result in a lockup situation, where the system must be replaced or the requirement change cannot be processed. Transformation capability is essential for open systems, as they must be able to adapt to changes in system specification.

Cyber Contingency Practice: Variance and Deviation

The preceding section explored which kind of cyber contingency exists in theory. Something different, and much more relevant, is the question of which kind of cyber contingency exists in practice, that is, for a given IACS installation. Many times, this question cannot be answered. Even though many asset owners are aware that cyber affects the reliability of their operations as much as electrical current, few take the effort to measure and evaluate critical cyber parameters. Is best case realistic for a given IACS installation? What is "typical" for a given environment? How big is de-facto deviation from target? How big is the safety margin left? Few asset owners can answer questions like these based on empirical evidence, because de-facto variation, or variance, of cyber parameters is rarely measured, monitored, and analyzed. In quality engineering it is well known that a process will not always produce product within quality tolerance margins. Therefore it is common practice to empirically verify variation around quality targets. Interestingly, this is very rarely done for cyber. On the other hand, experience does show that in real life, there is often considerable deviation from specification targets. This does often lead to situations where plant planners, operators, and maintenance engineers have a mind model of the system which no longer matches reality.

Examination of Netflow logs reveals that critical systems are accessed by all kinds of nonauthorized systems for reasons that might not even be determinable.

Network monitoring reveals that throughput and latency are considerably different from specification/best case. [Bryan Singer (2010) was the first to point out that network QoS should be monitored as an OEE loss factor.]

Inspection of computer systems reveals that many other applications are hosted than what is required per specification for said systems, some of which may be completely counterproductive (such as media players, IRC clients, unauthorized VNC servers, etc.).

A "walkaround audit" reveals that contractors use several other means of remote access than what is company policy, such as unauthorized dial-in modems.

An administrator "finds" obsolete operating system versions on various systems, deactivated antivirus software, missing AV signature updates, etc.

Inspection of a computer system reveals that the system is equipped with a network interface, and connected to a LAN, while per policy it shouldn't. Examination shows that the network interface card was once installed by a maintenance engineer to perform a software update, and was subsequently left installed and operational in the system.

During a cyber security risk assessment, a group of PLCs attached to a specific DCS server used another network protocol (H1) than what was expected (RFC1006). The asset owner was more than surprised about this finding, as he had ordered a reconfiguration months earlier. A contractor had already billed the change and had received payment for it.

The same type of application is running on multiple systems with different operating system versions (patch levels, etc.)

A maintenance engineer discovers that the same software application is installed and used in different versions and configurations on multiple systems.

A review of backup procedures reveals that several other ("creative") technical procedures are used than what is required by policy, and that some semicritical systems are not backed up at all.

Many control system engineers would be surprised to see what's actually happening in their cyberspace. A more unpleasant surprise is waiting if variance reaches a cyber tripwire, and output behavior, i.e., the behavior of the governed process, takes a "surprising" turn. (Examples are given in Appendix A.) Unfortunately, some maintenance engineers may avoid gathering empirical data on cyber variation because they fear that such data could force them to do something about the observed variance. If such data is not collected, one may bury his head in the sand and claim ignorance.

When discussing how to utilize a new system and procedure to test the network resilience of automation peripherals at a company which uses several thousand such systems from many different vendors, a control system engineer, internally blessed with "specialist" status for the technology in question, argues against using such checks in general. If a specific product failed the test, he would have to do something about it, because any other behavior would be reckless. What's the missing logical link here?

To get a picture of where the cyber tripwires of a given installation are, the following parameters should be established for all cyber parameters and all systems.

Legitimate value range and target value as specified. Example: The identity, or the number of systems that, according to specification, should exchange data with the SUC.

Potential variation as technically possible. Example: The identity or number of systems that technically can send data to the SUC (in case of system failures, accidental misaddressing, malicious activity, etc.). These limits are not identical with specification limits or control limits; they simply define the universe (or spectrum) of variation that is technically possible for this variable—for example, all systems connected to a given network segment.

Actual variation as observed. Example: The identity or number of systems that actually interchange data with the SUC, as verified by monitoring of network traffic for a given time frame.

Given the immense efforts that most operations take to determine the deviation of product characteristics from set specification targets as part of their routine quality engineering, it is sometimes surprising to see that the cyber aspects of control are left completely unmonitored, unreported, and unanalyzed. Where monitoring is done, it usually shows that deviation from the target level is substantial. It is then worthwhile to consider whether variance can be limited by tightening the technical spectrum limits, as will be discussed in the next chapter, in Section 3.3.

It is important to remember that installations with unknown, unmonitored, and undocumented cyber constraints are fragile per se. If such installations experience cyber-related problems, these problems usually come as a surprise, even though they are anything but surprising.

2.5   Fragile Control

To understand why and how cyber contingency may become a problem, it is instructive to look at the implementation and execution of control logic in a hypothetical system or a subsystem in isolation. For the purpose of this book, *control logic* is defined as the algorithmic relationship between controlling variables and controlled variables as observed experimentally. In a nutshell, the approach discussed here is similar to the concept of process capability, which is familiar to asset owners who apply statistical process control (SPC).

Problem #1: Control Logic with Unrestricted Input/ Output Mapping

Table 2-2 lists various combinations of controlling and controlled variables. Here, *valid* (with respect to input and output) is defined as being within limits of specification and implementation. The distinction between specification and implementation is important because implementation may not be in accordance with specification.

Table 2-2   Input/Output Combinations

	Valid Output	Invalid Output
Valid input	1. Undetermined; may be robust, may be fragile	2. Defective
Invalid input	3. Robust	4. Fragile

The possible input/output combinations as listed in the table may be interpreted as follows.

1. The valid input/valid output relation says little about the exercised degree of control. Commercial IACS products from established vendors beyond version 1.0 can reasonably be expected to perform to specification; otherwise the product (or the vendor) would probably go out of market.

2. A system that transforms valid input into invalid output is defective.

3. A system that prevents invalid input from resulting in invalid output is robust.

4. A system that transforms invalid input into invalid output is not necessarily defective, but it is definitely fragile. Cyber fragility is characterized by a function that yields correct results for valid input but undesired output for variations of valid input, even if such variations are typical for the given target environment. This is comparable to the classic "garbage in/garbage out" problem in IT.

The lesson here is that the behavior of a system for valid input says nothing about its fragility or robustness: It simply tells whether the system can be regarded as functional or defective. Whether the "input" in question is a malformed command sent via the network, a corrupt entry in a configuration file, or a "wrong" firmware image, what makes a system robust is its ability to prevent invalid output. A functional installation or product may still be unsatisfactory because of its fragility, and the robustness of a product may never be appreciated if the product never experiences contingency conditions.

What "valid input" means is defined largely by implementation. Even though implementation behavior may be verified against specification by testing a system with full-range input variation, this is rarely done. The distinction of valid versus invalid is not restricted to data content (= functional layer); it also applies to timing, context, and other cyber contingency layers as discussed earlier. Examples for different settings are given in Appendix A.

A system with a network command interface that allows for read operations (memory locations, Web pages, sensor values, etc.) will deliver valid output if the network command is well formed and the parameter(s) can be processed by the control logic. If the parameter(s) cannot be processed, several alternatives are possible: The system may respond with an error message; the system may simply ignore the command; or the system may crash or otherwise show unpredictable behavior ("garbage out").

Robustness is determined by negative testing. A system that is only tested positively may be functional but fragile. This observation extends beyond control logic. Systems that have become so complex that they are not fully testable anymore because of combinatorial explosion can hardly be robust.

- **Fragility criterion:** Control logic that does not yield desired output for the full variation range of controlling variables is fragile.
- **Potential loss-of-control situation:** Invalid input puts the system under consideration in an undesired state beyond specification. If an acceptable input range is not specified, this situation may not be preventable by the operator.

Problem #2: Sensitivity to Cyber Noise

A well-known problem from classic control theory is the sensitivity of output behavior to factors other than input signal and control factors. In parameter design, such factors are called noise factors (Taguchi and Chowdhury, 2005). A similar problem exists with respect to cyber, where output behavior may be less than 100% determined by control input. Even if the control input/output mapping is implemented in a robust manner by control logic, control output may still be sensitive to factors other than control input and unauthorized control paths (see below). This problem is frequently observed with networked automation peripherals.

> There have been many instances where IACS showed abnormal behavior during or after being hit by a network scan (ICMP packets, TCP SYNs, empty UDP packets), a broadcast packet, a DoS attack, etc., both in the lab and in real installations.

Cyber noise factors extend beyond online data. For example, slight changes in the execution environment, such as the application of operating system security patches, may also qualify as cyber noise if the behavior of the control system is sensitive to it. A practical problem with cyber noise is that it cannot be defined and determined in relation to specified standards.

Cyber noise is system/implementation specific. For example, when looking at data transmission at the transport layer, cyber noise may consist of completely well-formed and legitimate packets, such as broadcasts, network scans, etc., which may still cause a specific system or software process to fail or functionally degrade. Since such packets are typical for many networks, this is a classic example of cyber fragility.

Whether sensitivity to cyber noise is considered a product defect or not is not a technical but a legal question. It ultimately depends on the buying contract and on vendor/customer culture. Sensitivity to cyber noise is one of the most important and most interesting aspects of networked peripherals and IT systems, and it is surprising that, so far, no clear rules, legislation, standards, or ethics have emerged to deal with this problem.

- **Fragility criterion:** A control system that delivers undesired output in the presence of cyber noise is fragile.
- **Potential loss-of-control situation:** Even though it is receiving proper and legitimate commands, the system does not execute because it malfunctions due to being exposed to cyber noise.

2.6   Control Clouds

While the preceding section discussed problems that are rooted inside an individual control system and its capabilities to deal with cyber variation, there is yet another group of problems that is associated with the fact that in contemporary industrial installations, control is no longer executed in standalone systems—and also extending the proprietary barriers of a self-contained DCS.

For the purpose of this book, *control* is defined as the capability to continuously force output parameters depending on input parameters and control logic. In a closed-loop architecture, this is achieved by reading the value of a controlled variable, checking it against the appropriate target value according to control logic, making adjustments to the controlled variable, and reiterating the cycle. In digital control networks, it is not so easy. Figure 2-6 illustrates a typical system design for a PLC that is communicating with a SCACA client/server application via an OPC server. Control still seems to be executed locally in the PLC, but the reality is that other systems in the process control network have an opportunity to change setpoints, ladder logic, runtime environment (via firmware uploads), or even force outputs by applying legitimate commands. So while the idea may still be that control is executed locally, systems in the control cloud technically have full command authority and will usually take advantage of it to optimize the process. The term *control cloud* is used here to express that there is no longer one dedicated endpoint for any sensor or actuator in this network, but countless anonymous systems that might be located anywhere. The inside of a control cloud is foggy. Unidentified systems and agents may establish ad-hoc interaction with other systems and thereby alter output behavior in a way that no longer follows any planned, documented, and traceable procedure.

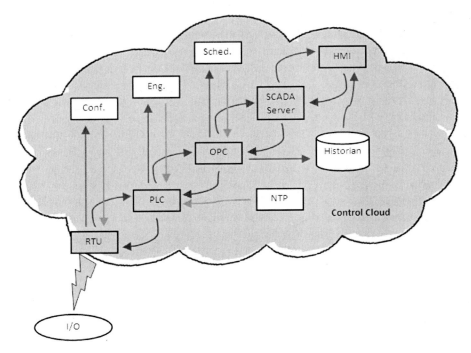

Figure 2-6   A control cloud. The main control path moves through the shaded systems. In addition to the systems depicted in the cloud, other systems may influence process control, either directly or indirectly.

Different from a control loop, control is executed in an IACS network via a *control path* by passing messages via the network. This path is created by transmitting sensor inputs and process variables as well as commands as digital messages. During transmission, such messages usually pass through various systems, software processes, and network components.

Figure 2-6 shows a situation which is typical for modern IACS networks. I/O is hardwired to a RTU which is attached to a process control network that may use protocols such as Modbus/TCP, Ethernet/IP, or Profinet. The RTU is commanded by a PLC with which it interchanges digital commands and responses. The PLC is accessed by a SCADA server by means of an OPC server in between. The SCADA server is accessed by an HMI terminal. This is the *main control path*. Besides the beaten path, other applications may interfere with I/O as well, both indirectly and directly. For example, a logistics scheduler, material management application, or OEE software might talk directly to the OPC server to access process variables. An engineering workstation will usually talk directly to the PLC to upload optimized ladder logic, or for diagnostic and debugging purposes. And a configuration utility might access the RTU directly to upload new firmware, or for configuration changes. Inside the control cloud, there are yet other components, such as an NTP server which provides the time of day for the PLC, and a historian which is fed by the OPC server and accessed by an operator's terminal (HMI). The following aspects are worth considering.

- The diagram in Figure 2-6 is simplified. In real life, interaction may be much more complex, if only because there may be hundreds or even thousands of RTUs, PLCs, and operator panels in a single installation, which may interfere with each other.
- The length of the control path, expressed in the number of hops, is not predetermined or fixed. There may be an arbitrary number of systems in between. A control path may even extend through the Internet, as is customary for remote access by contractors, which may even be located on a different continent. Alternate routes and detours may be taken, and not just with respect to network gear.
- There is no end-to-end reliability of the control path. Messages may get lost or altered without the sender or receiver noticing.
- There may be multiple concurrent control paths.
- Control paths may originate from anonymous, perhaps even illegitimate sources.

Such design introduces several major reliability problems that may lead to loss of control, as will be explained below.

Problem #1: Multiple Control Paths (Shared Command and Configuration Authority)

Multiple control inputs present a challenge for control, as this opens up the chance for control conflicts, along with the question of who (either a human being or a technical system) has command authority. This presents a real problem for networked IACS installations, where many systems in the network may send legitimate commands to a specific IACS, sometimes even remotely via the Internet.

The shared control authority problem is well known from aircraft control, where two-seat cockpits are usually equipped with dual control yokes or sticks. In case of control conflicts, the stronger pilot will win where mechanical controls are used. For fly-by-wire systems, the situation is different. Here, control inputs from both sticks are consolidated by the flight control system, which has already led to problems when at least one of the pilots was not aware of additional control input. Therefore, sidesticks have been equipped with takeover pushbuttons so that control authority is limited to one input. If the takeover pushbutton is pushed again at the other sidestick, the rule is that the last one wins, which is similar to a cyber environment in which the last command overrides previous commands.

In fly-by-wire aircraft, the crew enjoys the luxury of being able to communicate directly, face to face, and there are visual and aural indicators when there areconcurrent control inputs, and in the situation of forced control takeover from pressing the takeover pushbutton. In IACS installations, the situation is more complicated. There is no indication of multiple control inputs, which may even originate remotely. This is comparable to an airplane control input issued by a crew member in the galley, or even by a passenger. Compared to office IT, this would be similar to any system in the network, including contractors, being technically able to manipulate a specific printout or spreadsheet cell content without the originator even noticing. While in IT this would perhaps be regarded as unacceptable, in the ICS world, it is the norm—even where consequences may be much more severe.

For the sake of flexibility, shared (networked) command and configuration interfaces have largely been viewed as a benefit. Therefore many installations exist where RTUs, controllers, PLCs, DDE servers, OPC servers, and proprietary command interfaces are network-accessible by multiple systems without any means of authentication and authorization. In such architectures, the potential for control conflict, and the principal question of command authority, is ignored. No matter how this problem is viewed, remote and shared control input/command authority require access control and monitoring by the operator (as the ultimate authority)—otherwise system behavior cannot be predicted.

- **Fragility criterion:** Shared control input/command authority which can result in undesired output must be considered fragile.

- **Potential loss-of-control situation:** Commands of operator A are "overwritten" by operator B (or any anonymous software process, including malware) with access to the command interface of the system under consideration. Operator A experiences loss of control.

Problem #2: Undetected Broken Control Paths

A major cause of the 2003 East Coast power blackout was a loss of view which was not recognized by operators. "Starting around 14:14 EDT, FE's control room operators lost the alarm function that provided audible and visual indications when a significant piece of equipment changed from an acceptable to a problematic condition. Shortly thereafter, the EMS system lost a number of its remote control consoles. Next it lost the primary server computer that was hosting the alarm function, and then the backup server such that all functions that were being supported on these servers were stopped at 14:54 EDT. However, for over an hour no one in FE's control room grasped that their computer systems were not operating properly, even though FE's Information Technology support staff knew of the problems and were working to solve them, and the absence of alarms and other symptoms offered many clues to the operators of the EMS system's impaired state. . . . Analysis of the alarm problem performed by FE suggests that the alarm process essentially 'stalled' while processing an alarm event, such that the process began to run in a manner that failed to complete the processing of that alarm or produce any other valid output (alarms). In the meantime, new inputs—system condition data that needed to be reviewed for possible alarms—built up in and then overflowed the process' input buffers." (U.S.-Canada Power System Outage Task Force, 2003)

This is a classic example of a broken control path without any of the endpoint systems (or humans) noticing. While both the alarm-generating sensors and the operators sitting in the control room were functional, the alarms were never processed, and loss of view wasn't even recognized (until the auxiliary power units of control room equipment kicked in due to loss of grid power).

- **Fragility criterion:** A control system with requirements and dependencies that do not match the intended operating environment over the planned lifecycle or which are simply not known is fragile.
- **Potential loss-of-control situation:** The system under consideration does not execute valid commands when resource limits are reached, when required services are unavailable, or when the runtime environment has been changed.

Problem #3: Undetected Message Alteration

For the sake of modularity and software reuse, some control system architectures allow for easy message alteration that is not detected by the sender and receiver. An example is the man-in-the-middle attack for alteration of ladder logic that was used by Stuxnet.

> *Stuxnet exploited the product architecture of the attacked controller by hijacking the vendor's driver DLL. The driver DLL is used by both the development environment and the SCADA product from the same vendor. By placing itself between the development application and the legitimate driver DLL, Stuxnet was able to modify ladder logic sent to and received from the controller without either the development application or the controller noticing.*

- **Fragility criterion:** A control system architecture that allows for message alteration that cannot be detected is fragile.
- **Potential loss-of-control situation:** The system under consideration executes illegitimate control logic without being recognized.

Problem #4: Antistructure Attractors and Application Interlocks

A cloud in the sky needs condensation nuclei to form. Humidity in the air can only condensate around such nuclei, which are in essence little particles of dust. Something similar can be observed with control clouds, where we find *attractors* around which software processes and data flow sticks to form foggy antistructure (i.e., disorder and chaos). Such attractors are, for example, general-purpose network services such as SMB/CIFS file shares, NFS, DCOM, or FTP. These services are so flexible that one can do so much with them without planning. They attract ill-designed architectures and software processes which at some point will present a major problem for maintainability, usually years after installation. They also attract malware. Looking at the traffic and content of any shared directory, OPC server, or FTP server years after deployment usually is like looking at a water hole in the savannah: It is populated by all kinds of wild animals.

> *One of the main means of distribution for the Stuxnet malware is shared folders. This is not an accident. The creators of Stuxnet*

were well aware that shared folders are used abundantly in typical target environments. Cyber condensation nuclei are so irresistible that they even attract cyber warriors.

Problems can even get bigger if antistructure attractors are used to interconnect different applications or application subroutines. Similar to database servers, shared folders have often been abused for interprocess communication, resulting in complex fragile systems that may prove difficult to make robust.

Chapter 3

Cyber Robustness

The characteristics of cyber fragility that were identified earlier provide a good starting point for exploring and establishing just the opposite: cyber robustness. Cyber fragility is not rooted in technological problems; it is rooted in flaws of human behavior. Fragility can be largely eliminated by proper planning, testing, and documentation in the design and maintenance phase, and in procedures that limit variation in the operational phase. Fragility leads to problems if the people responsible for designing/planning and operating an IACS installation choose to live with insufficient system understanding and documentation. Fragility or robustness is a deliberate choice, whether conscious or not. The following sections illustrate how robustness can be established and maintained once this decision has been made.

3.1   Cyber Robustness Defined

Robustness is the ability to continue normal operation despite contingencies, the ability to withstand changes in procedure or circumstance, and the ability to cope with variations in the operating environment with minimal or no damage, alteration, or loss of functionality. A robust system or process is insensitive to variation to the greatest extent possible. As will be explained later, a robust system is also a secure system: a system that is prepared to withstand even aggressive cyber attacks of the Stuxnet variety.

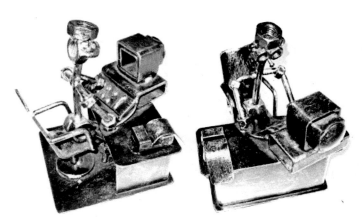

Figure 3-1   A robust structure. Unlike the house of cards shown in Chapter 1, this structure will easily survive a blower attack, or a drop from the table. (Courtesy of Guido Menebröcker.)

Figure 3-1 shows Sammy, the office clerk, sitting at his computerized desk. (The structure itself is sitting on one of the author's clients' desk and is about 6 inches tall. The author confesses that his thoughts were sometimes captured by the amazing craftsmanship of this structure while discussing complex control software issues with the client.) The pieces that the structure is composed of are solidly welded together. One can even hammer (moderately) on the structure without damaging it. Furthermore, all pieces used are standard equipment that can be purchased at any hardware shop. Should Sammy someday get a nice flat-screen monitor to replace the old CRT, the update would go quite smoothly. Changing any detail (or subsystem) can be accomplished with all other parts of the structure remaining intact. Pretty robust!

The desire to build robust systems is often rooted in the insight that it is virtually impossible to predict externalities that could potentially influence system behavior. Based on this insight, the goal of robustness is to design and operate systems with reliable behavior even in the face of nonanticipated circumstances.

Cyber Robustness Axioms

1. *Any IACS component, system, or installation should be considered to function only under the parameters and circumstances specified, tested, and documented.* The fact that a vendor or operator does not

provide any specification (or even documentation) about the cyber aspects of a system should be treated as an indication of fragility.

2. *Robustness is verifiable.* The fragility or robustness of IACS can be verified empirically by negative testing, given that system complexity does not preclude exhaustive testing (combinatorial explosion).

3. *The more complexity, the higher the effort to design and operate a robust system. Any additional degree of freedom will make a system more fragile.* Fragility is a price for flexibility and complexity. Adding cyber complexity is easy; making it robust is difficult. While it may be tempting for vendors to incorporate more and more cyber features into IACS products, there is a trade-off in reliability and maintainability.

4. *The most prominent indication of a fragile system or installation is inadequate system understanding, evidenced by lack of documentation.*

5. *The longer the projected lifetime of a system, the higher the robustness requirements.* If for nothing else, simply because of the long average lifetime for IACS, the robustness requirements are higher than for short-lived systems such as those found in office IT or in home use.

6. *The robustness or fragility of a system cannot be determined by looking at components in isolation, but only by viewing the system's function and interaction with its environment.* Variation is not a property of the system, but of the interaction with the system's environment. Robustness is a behavioral property.

7. *Robustness is independent of variation cause (malicious attack, accidental misconfiguration, random failure, etc.) and type of consequence (health, environment, availability, etc.).* Robustness is defined with respect to specification conformant behavior under variation, where the most important area is the type of cyber variation which is typical for the target environment, because this is what can be expected to materialize with the highest probability. Robustness is different from fault tolerance because factors that can affect the behavior of fragile cyber systems may not necessarily be considered faults. Such factors include erroneous user input, failure of network equipment, planned change, or malware.

8. *Cyber robustness and fragility manifest in a system's reliability and maintainability.* A system per se, in a static view, is not subject to cyber variation. Robustness and fragility can only be determined with respect to specified and experimentally observed system behavior.

9. *Robustness is not about using specific technology, it is about proper use of technology.* It is about the mastership of process control, and

about designing, operating, and verifying robust systems and procedures. It is a discipline rather than a technology.

10. *Design fragility may be compensated by compensating controls and operational procedures.* In the same manner as a device with IP protection class 00 may still be used in a humid and dusty environment if external protection is provided, IACS with fragile design may still be used in a robust manner if operational procedures prevent operational cyber limits from being reached.

Robustification

At their core, fragility and robustness are not technical problems or challenges. It is no technical challenge to design, implement, and operate robust cyber systems; it is not even particularly demanding, and it is not necessarily expensive.

Robustification is the discipline of planning and designing robust systems, and of operating systems in a robust manner. Cyber robustification is not a technology; it's a discipline that can be acquired and taught, and the results of its application can be measured and evaluated. To achieve or enhance cyber robustness, it is not necessary to incorporate a new technology, to get rid of specific existing technology, or to buy specific products.

The behavior of every IACS is sensitive to variation in operating conditions such as electrical current and environmental conditions such as temperature, humidity, and dust. However, sensitivity is not limited to physical conditions; it also applies to cyber conditions which may include network connectivity, accessibility of specific services, and potentially impairing events such as a malware outbreak. While the application of best practices to make a system insensitive to the physical parameters of its operating environment is standard engineering practice, similar procedures to shield against cyber parameters are just emerging.

Robustification strategies can be built around limiting variation and/or tolerating variation—without making any predictions or assumptions about externalities, such as why, where, and when variation may occur. The basic approach of robustification is to reduce controllable variation (which is part of the system) and to make the system more tolerant of uncontrollable variation (which is part of the environment). A reliable engineering solution does not rely on uncontrolled factors. To reduce controllable variation, it is essential to understand that not all uncontrolled variation is uncontrollable. Variation within the system may be controllable to a large extent, whereas environmental variation and evolutional change generally are uncontrollable.

3.2   Robustification Theory: Principles

Based on the discussion of cyber fragility earlier, it is easy to identify weak spots in control system design and operation that can be eliminated. There are four basic robustification principles: the blockout principle, the avoid-mess principle, the consistency principle, and the AERA principle, which will all be explained in this section.

The Blockout Principle

As discussed earlier, the ultimate goal of control is to force the output of controlled variables with minimal variability. Looking at control in the classic input/control logic (transfer function)/output model, it is easy to see that there are three areas where robustification can be applied. (Note: In this section the term *controller* is not used, as the same applies to software processes running on IT hardware systems with general-purpose operating systems.)

To illustrate the different areas, in Figure 3-2 the classic model of a simple controller is used, with input and output visualized as cones to indicate variability. Robustification efforts can be applied to input, execution system, and output. For the purpose of simplifying our discussion, we can even limit the problem to prevent out-of-bounds output values. In principle, out-of-bounds output values may be caused by out-of-bounds input values, and by a processing function that transfers out-of-bounds input values to out-of-bounds output values.

- If out-of-bounds input is blocked, the chances for out-of-bounds output are reduced.
- If the execution of invalid input is blocked within the execution system, chances for out-of-bounds output is also reduced. The same applies to efforts assuring the integrity of the execution system (for example, checking whether a firmware image that is loaded on a controller is legitimate and uncorrupted).

Figure 3-2   The classic model.

- As a last resort, out-of-bounds output may be blocked by external logic and procedure.

These principles are so important that they are further illustrated in Table 3-1. In addition to the input/processing/output model, there is also a

Table 3-1　Summary of Blockout Principles

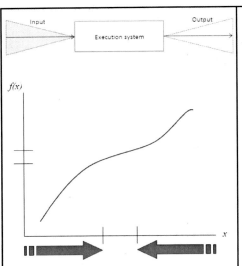

	Blockout subprinciple #1: Blocking invalid input. If invalid input can be fed to the controller (execution system), variability in output may occur. By eliminating invalid input (not only digital, but with respect to other cyber contingency layers as well), the chance for invalid output decreases. Strategies how this can be implemented include: • Reducing network exposure • Limiting user access
	Blockout subprinciple #2: Limiting transfer function range. The second area where robustification may be applied is the execution system. Even if invalid input is fed to the system, it does not necessarily have to result in invalid output. Successful strategies that implement this principle include: • System hardening • Reducing general-purpose software and services • Inherent safety • Resilient code and architecture • Code execution and configuration tamper control • Encoding meta information

(*Continued on following page*)

Table 3-1   (*Continued*)

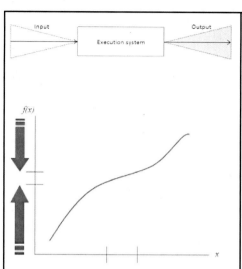	**Blockout subprinciple #3: Blocking invalid output.** The third area where robustification may be applied is the reduction of output variability. Here it is assumed that, for whatever reason, the execution system eventually produces invalid output. Attempts are made to prevent this from materializing in process behavior by alerting operators in time, or by shutting down the process in situations when invalid output may be worse than no output at all. Well-established strategies in this area are • Monitoring and alarming • Safeguards

function graph which is intended to clarify the focus of the robustification principle in question.

The blockout principles may be applied not only in isolation, they may be combined in the same system, which leads us to the robustification theorem of combinatorial leverage.

> **Robustification theorem of combinatorial leverage:** Combining blockout principles for one and the same system may result in disproportional increases of robustness.

Combinatorial leverage is important because in real life, many system aspects cannot be made robust to the desired level by applying just one principle. Combining blockout principles may then do the trick.

> *Reducing general-purpose network interfaces such as DCOM may reach a limit because their functionality is required by software such as OPC servers. Reducing system accessibility (network reachability, authentication procedures) may then provide for the additional amount of input variability reduction.*

This tactic will be discussed more thoroughly in Chapters 6 and 7.

The Avoid-Mess Principle

The avoid-mess principle is the principle of avoiding undocumented, quick-and-dirty, spaghetti-code interlocking applications and antistructure attractors. This principle has been well known in software engineering for decades, and there are libraries full of books that have been written about it. The automation world may have to learn the hard way that structuring and documenting code, data, and data flow are essential to cope with growing complexity. The lesson may, however, be much more costly than in IT, as it involves installations and processes that cannot be changed in a matter of months because they are interlocked with actual machinery and physical processing.

It is not difficult to convince anybody of the advantages of having clean and documented code and cyber architecture. It may be very difficult, though, to convince management to supply the required resources in terms of personnel, staff time, and education to make it happen. As long as cyber is regarded as an add-on to "real" engineering, things are not likely to change here. It can be projected that sooner or later the exorbitant maintenance cost of unstructured "local" solutions will force a change in engineering culture.

The Consistency Principle

The blockout principle applies to individual systems viewed in isolation. A real installation, however, may consist of thousands of such systems, along with operating and maintenance procedures which are performed day by day, or hundred times per day, by different systems or different people in the organization, over a lifespan of many years. For a real-world installation, it is easy to understand that robustifying a single system in a lab environment doesn't help much. It may be a good starting point, but the effort will be wasted if it isn't transformed into a consistent system architecture or operating procedure.

As is well known from quality engineering, it is disadvantageous to solve the same task by different tools or procedures. From a robustification point of view, the major aspect to focus on is nonrequired variation. Where systems and procedures fulfill the same function and serve the same purpose, it is desirable to use identical types and versions of systems, configurations, and identical procedures. Consistency should be established with respect to multiplicity, and to repetitions. The consistency principle is very much related to establishing company or even industry standards. It applies well to the following areas:

- Subsystems/components that perform identical or similar tasks (consistency in technology, architecture, make and model, product type, version, configuration, execution environment, etc.). Inconsistency may lead to problems such as "It runs on some systems, but not on others," version conflicts, and maintenance efforts higher than necessary.
- Application-neutral automated procedures for identical or similar purposes, such as automated backup.
- Nonautomated procedures for identical or similar purposes, such as manual backup or remote access.

Basically, this is an essential quality principle that has been established in many companies for decades, especially in companies that are ISO 9000 certified. There is little reason why this principle should not be applied to industrial automation and control systems and procedures—as always in quality, empirical verification of consistency should be mandated.

The consistency principle goes far beyond preventing individual cyber trips. It is an important building block for any organization that intends to incorporate a sustainable robustification strategy. Sustainability can only be achieved if optimizations that have been developed for single prototypic systems and procedures are transformed into intraorganizational standards that govern procurement and the training of new employees.

The AERA Principle (Adequate Execution Resources Allocation)

The principles discussed so far are conceptual, or "virtual." They will, however, barely produce a robust installation on their own. Though virtual, cyber only exists when executed on real, physical systems with real performance limitations by real people with real time constraints and education limits. What's worse, as has been highlighted earlier in the section on control clouds, *resource demands may be difficult to determine because of hidden dependencies.* This is the area where binary and analog cyber contingency tends to exhibit—where systems simply fail or degrade with surprising side effects.

The most prominent approaches for adequate resource allocation are

- Physical redundancy
- Physical performance reserves
- Allocation and organization of sufficient personnel (establishing responsibilities, service-level agreements, etc.)

3.3   Robustification Practice: Strategies

The principles explained above are intended to provide an understanding of how and why robustification works in theory. Applying robustification to real systems is another story, one that may be performed better using a slightly different, more practical approach. In that approach, the four principles and their subprinciples are put into a different perspective that is centered on the question of how to impose and enforce structure on complex systems. For practical considerations, the following three categories can be used:

> **Reduction strategies (imposing structure).** Reduction strategies aim at reducing, restricting, or eliminating functionality that is not required for the system's purpose as specified. Reduction of variation is virtually identical to simplifying or *structuring* the system under consideration. Reduction strategies are "passive" and materialize mostly in design. Think about it as building a highway system for a specific county. The basic idea is to have traffic flow smoothly on as little asphalt with as few intersections as possible. What previously was a mess of back-country roads, many of them unpaved and known only to locals, is to be replaced by structured concrete that makes traffic flow much more efficiently and safely.

> **Surplus strategies (enforcing and reinforcing structure).** Surplus strategies aim at enhancing, duplicating, or enriching functionality that is not required for normal operations under ideal circumstances, but extends the system's reliability in case of contingencies. Surplus strategies are "active" and usually imply purchase and installation of extra equipment and/or procedures that would normally not be required. In the highway construction example, this would be like enhancing the highway system with road shoulders, toll booths, gas stations, rest areas, and radar speed checks. None of these would be necessary if everything was going according to plan.

> **Change management (modifying structure).** Change management aims at establishing an organized process for managing forced and planned variation, or change (change in requirements, change in specification, end-of-lifetime). While the necessity for change management is well understood in office IT, it is nonexistent on some plant floors, with notable exceptions especially in the chemical industry and in pharmaceuticals. In the highway construction example, this would be like installing signs to signal detours around construction zones, building new exits, establishing speed lanes, etc.

Differences and Similarities Between Reduction and Surplus

Reduction and surplus strategies are not opposed to each other, as one may be tempted to think at first. Actually, the same strategy may be regarded a reduction strategy for one installation and a surplus strategy for another. For example, where network switches limit traffic based on access control lists (ACLs), reducing network traffic is a reduction strategy, whereas in another installation where network gear does not support filtering and firewalls must be installed to do the job, the same strategy will be viewed as surplus.

Surplus strategies and reduction strategies feature two independent dimensions, as illustrated in Figure 3-3, where feature set and flexibility define the vertical axis and variation defines the horizontal axis. In theory, a specific IACS implementation may feature basic functionality with heavy or little surplus, or a rich feature set, again with heavy or little surplus. In reality, the reduction and surplus characteristics of any given IACS product usually can be grouped into typical boxes, as shown in Figure 3-3:

- The upper left quadrant is populated by the bulk of commercial off-the-shelf systems. Such systems usually have a rich feature set but little ability to deal with cyber variation.

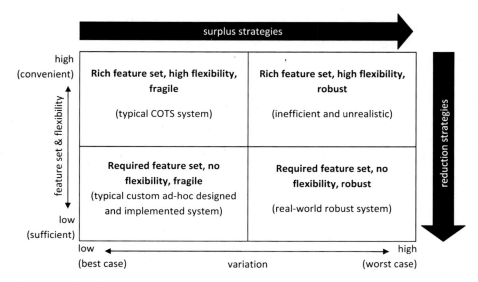

Figure 3-3   Surplus and reduction strategies.

- The lower left quadrant (small feature set, tolerating little or no variation) is populated with custom ad-hoc designed and implemented systems. In-house developers and contractors usually don't spend much
  time or creativity on nonrequired functionality (as they understand it in
  the absence of written specification), because the priority is on getting
  the job done in the shortest time possible. Real-world robust systems
  can be found in the lower right quadrant, where both reduction strategies and surplus strategies have been applied.

- Systems with a rich feature set and a high level of reserves (upper
  right quadrant) are usually not found in real life because the application of surplus strategies comes with a price. Providing resources that
  aren't used or needed most of the time does not make sense for nice-
  to-have functions.

- The lower right quadrant contains robust systems that can be found in the
  real world, where the feature set has been reduced to bare necessities.

The Foundation: System Model and Specification

Robustification can only be applied based on a solid understanding and documentation of the system under consideration, its intended use, and its limits.
In the highway construction example above, an accurate map of the county
must be available before planning can even begin. In addition to a map, the
planner would be interested in knowing the endpoints (interfaces) of the
highway system, the projected traffic volume and type, etc. An accurate system model and specification is the foundation of any robust cyber system.

The system model and specification provide what one must *know* before
robustification principles can be applied. Robustification strategies tell
what one can *do* to increase robustness once that the system is modeled
and specified.

In a nutshell, system model and specification allow determination of what
is there, but not necessary (and may therefore be cut away by reduction strategies), and also determination of what is necessary, but not there (and must
be added by surplus strategies). System modeling and specification are so
important that both topics will be discussed in depth in separate chapters.

3.4   How to Approach Robustification Projects

While it might be desirable to go about robustification using a big-bang
approach, for any but the smallest installation this will hardly be possible
for practical reasons. The recommended strategy is to follow a grass-roots

approach, starting with small robustification nuclei and expanding them over time, with the long-term goal of making robustification part of the organization's culture, similar to quality engineering. So, while robustification should really be a continuous process anchored in company culture, the way to get there is by starting with small robustification projects. It is recommended to define robustification projects in a way that they can be completed within several weeks or several months. An important point that influences the success or failure of a robustification project is the definition of the target system or procedure, which will be highlighted below. It might also help to split a robustification project into several phases, such as (1) documentation and concept, (2) prototype system, and (3) rollout, stretching a more complex robustification project over more than a year, but still keeping individual phases well below a year.

Picking a Good Robustification Target

To a large extent, the outlook for success of a robustification project is determined by a good or bad choice of the target. For this reason, guidelines are given as to how to pick a good target for a robustification project. An easy heuristic for identifying good robustification candidates is to look at the impact that the robustification project will have for the organization. Such impact can be expressed by the number of effected systems, multiplied by the projected remaining lifetime, expressed in *system years*:

$$\text{Robustification impact} = \text{number of effected systems} \\ \times \text{projected remaining lifetime in years}$$

When counting the number of affected systems for a potential robustification candidate, hidden dependencies should be taken into account. Application-neutral infrastructure usually has an impact on a large number of systems. Examples are database servers, backup servers, Active Directory servers, and remote access gateways.

If in doubt about the best choice among several robustification project candidates, Pareto analysis can help, as is customary in total production maintenance (TPM). While TPM is concerned with identifying loss factors, we are interested in identifying project gain factors. The following example illustrates how this can be done. From the large variety of systems in a specific sample organization, we have picked the following:

- 300 near-identical operator terminals with a projected remaining lifetime of 6 years

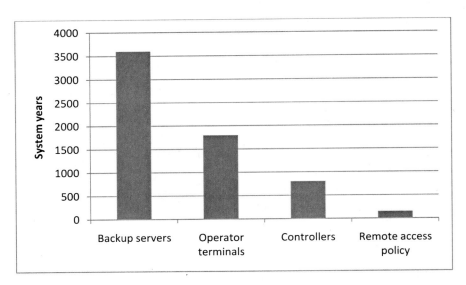

Figure 3-4   Comparison of system years.

- 5 backup servers that serve 1,200 computer systems, with a projected remaining lifetime of 3 years
- 400 near-identical controllers with a projected remaining lifetime of 2 years
- A remote access policy that affects 50 systems and is intended to be in place for 3 years

To compare these, system years are computed. For this simple example, it is not even necessary to draw a Pareto chart, but it is done anyway to illustrate the concept (see Figure 3-4).

As was easy to guess, the backup servers look like the most rewarding target for a robustification project, followed by the operator terminals.

Robustifying Nonexisting Systems

The impact equation can even be applied to planned systems, and to procedures, such as policies or standard operating procedures. The best targets are those that don't even exist yet, meaning that they are in the planning or procurement stage. Such targets offer the following advantages:

- Projected lifetime is usually longer than for existing systems.
- Design changes can be made without painstaking modifications to actual production environments.

- Documentation can be demanded by the vendor rather than having to reverse-engineer a system for producing documentation.

Every organization is a living organism. For any asset owner, focusing only on the robustification of existing systems may never lead the organization to a meaningful level of robustness if there is a constant stream of new fragile systems pouring onto the plant floor every month. The most promising strategy is to stop this leak first.

For a long-term robustification strategy, the number of new systems per month (or year) is essential for determining the robustification effort required to reduce overall fragility and to achieve sustainability. For example, if the organization is installing 5,000 new cyber systems per year but only manages to robustify 3,000 systems per year, overall fragility will increase despite robustification efforts. If the organization manages to robustify 5,000 systems per year, and puts all effort on robustifying new systems, it may still take many years until the last fragile legacy system is put out of service. If the same organization focuses on robustifying existing legacy systems, sustainability may never be achieved with 5,000 new fragile systems hitting the plant floor every year. Bottom line: The biggest robustification efforts should go to planning and procurement. Personnel and budget allocated for robustification must be sufficient to robustify at least the annual number of new systems and procedures.

Robustifying Existing Systems

No matter how fragile it may be, a robustification effort for an unsuspicious legacy system might be wasted because of the prevalent "Never touch a running system" syndrome (see the Appendix). Usually, management has no sympathy for changing smoothly running processes, even when indications are that the slightest wisp of wind might disrupt the process.

The best opportunity to start a robustification project for existing systems is a change event. Such change events may be end-of-lifetime for a specific component or changing characteristics in the system's environment, such as going from RS-232 point-to-point connectivity to Ethernet.

3.5   Recommended Robustification Procedure

Once that a suitable target for a robustification project is selected, it is recommended to follow a five-step procedure, which will be repeated in subsequent chapters on robustification best practices. The five steps are as follows.

1. Document what you have

a. Produce the system documentation for the selected target:

- For the selected target, get the system documentation.

- If no documentation exists, acknowledge that you have a problem. Your robustification project will take much longer and may require additional authorization by management. Convince management that nonexisting technical system documentation is not an option in engineering, and that in a modern automation environment, not knowing about data flow and memory requirements is similar to not knowing about pipe locations and pressure tolerances. Don't accept undocumented systems and procedures. System documentation is so important that the whole next chapter is devoted to the subject.

- Documentation is not limited to existing systems and procedures. It may as well detail planned systems and procedures that are not yet implemented.

b. Verify the completeness and accuracy of the documentation:

- System documentation that is incomplete or outdated doesn't help much. Check the documentation's accuracy by empirically comparing it to real life (i.e., the actual system configuration). For procedures (such as policies and SOPs), check whether procedural descriptions are followed, and to what extent.

- For nonexisting targets in the design, planning, or procurement stage, accuracy cannot be checked against real life. However, the documentation can still be compared against requirements (see next step), and it can be determined wether the documented design is practical. Criteria for practicality, such as how much room the system model leaves for variation, will be discussed in a later chapter.

c. Update the documentation:

- Many times, the reality check of the existing documentation will identify inaccuracies. The documentation should then be updated to reflect the de-facto state of the real-world target.

2. Document what you need

a. Produce the specification for the target system:

- For the selected target, get the specification.

- If no *written* specification exists, this is proof of system fragility, since any variation of cyber parameters may lead the system to malfunction. Reliability with unknown system requirements and operating conditions is not achievable. If a specification must be written from scratch, this usually requires the help of technical subject-matter experts. However, writing a specification usually requires much less time and effort than producing a system model.

b. Verify the completeness and accuracy of the specification:

- A specification should match a formal framework, which will be outlined in a subsequent chapter.

- Many existing specifications are incomplete and only touch areas that are believed not to be evident. However, experience shows that such evidence may exist only in the heads of a handful of engineers who are intimately familiar with the target. Completeness of a specification means that following the specification will produce a working solution, and a similar (at best, identical) solution if different people apply the specification.

- A predominant problem with incomplete specification is that vital dependencies are hidden and may therefore be overlooked in a robustification effort. For example, while items such as NTP servers or domain servers often are not listed in a system specification because they are considered self-evident, experience has shown that such seemingly trivial assets may contribute significantly to the fragility or robustness of a specific system.

- Technical verification of accuracy usually requires a subject-matter expert.

3. Identify and close the gaps

If you reach step 3, this is a good sign, since it says that you have a verified system model and a complete and accurate system specification. Both are building blocks for robustification.

a. Identify gaps between the system model and the specification:

If requirements and their implementation are specified, this can then be compared to the system model. This comparison is checked against the following criteria:

- *The target system/procedure does not meet material requirements.* A system that does not meet its technical requirements is fragile and unreliable by definition. Note: If it is not possible to establish whether the target fulfills requirements, because of nonexisting requirements, this is also an indication of a fragile and unreliable system (see above).

- *The target system/procedure does meet requirements, but it allows for alternative configurations with less variation.* The bulk of robustification work is not concerned with systems that don't meet requirements, as these rarely go into operation on real plant floors. Usually the more interesting angles for robustification are related to design optimization, where a specific requirement is fulfilled by an alternative implementation that still meets requirements but squeezes out variability.

b. Close the gaps:

- The next step is to close the observed gaps between what you have and what you need. Usually, there is more than one way this can be done. Many suggestions will be given in subsequent chapters that list best-practice approaches for robustification. For a non-existing target (design, planning, procurement), closing the gaps does not involve technical reconfiguration but is limited to changing the system model.

- Any changes must be checked for practicability and cost.

4. Document changes

Robustification changes a system or procedure. Performing such changes in an unstructured way may ultimately lead to less overall robustness than before. At the very least, the system or procedure documentation should be updated to reflect the changes. The better approach is, of course, to integrate robustification with an organized change management process that starts at step 1. A short review of change management is given in Chapter 8.

5. Pursue consistency and sustainability

Robustifying an isolated system is of little overall value for the organization. In accordance with the consistency principle mentioned above, it should be attempted to apply robustification changes to systems of identical or similar type; or, in the language terms of change mangagement, to "roll out" the change. The original target of the robustification project should be viewed as a prototype that now needs to be taken to real production in order to harvest the full benefit of robustification. In addition, the robustification project should be taken as a learning experience for optimizing the robustification process in the organization.

a. Target-specific efforts toward sustainability:

A "rollout" of a robustified system architecture is an essential leverage for getting the most out of robustification, since the concept work doesn't need to be repeated. It has already been accomplished and comes for free. Therefore, as highlighted above, targets with a large number of similar systems will yield the most in terms of cost-effectiveness. Promising targets include:

- Similar systems within the same facility
- Similar targets within other facilities of the same organization
- Procedures that are performed by many individuals, and/or are repeated over time

b. Generic efforts toward sustainability:

Every robustification project is a learning experience that allows the organization to optimize not only the dedicated target system but also the robustification process itself. The following suggestions indicate typical focus points that are generic.

- Try to establish an intraorganizational standard for documentation (system model and specification). This will make subsequent robustification projects much easier. Implementing a central document management system may help further.
- Establish estimates of how many other systems are undocumented and fragile; make suggestions for follow-up robustification projects.
- Determine how lessons learned in a robustification project can be integrated into the design, planning, and procurement of new systems.

Chapter 4

Building a System Model

There is only one thing worse than uncontrolled cyber variation and fragile control implementation: inadequate understanding of the system under consideration, indicated by the absence of an accurate, documented system model. Nevertheless, for many operators and maintenance engineers of highly automated complex plants, daily navigation through the cyber space of their automated production environment takes place in the dark. When no maps are available, even direction-finding gear such as a compass is of little use. Such maps would identify contingency zones and cyber tripwires. They would also suggest good places to impose and reinforce structure. They may also be an invaluable guideline for maintenance, be it with respect to troubleshooting of cyber-related malfunctions or with respect to system retrofits and migrations. System documentation using adequate and accurate models is so important and yet so rarely done properly that a whole chapter is dedicated to this topic.

An IACS network is a man-made technical system. It has not grown naturally, and if it appears as a miracle, this is not due to technology but to the people who designed, commissioned, documented (or failed to document), operate, and maintain the system. A system that is not fully understood cannot be reliable and poses a major problem for maintenance. Insufficient system understanding and lack of documentation will almost certainly result in unpleasant surprises, especially for systems with long lifetimes. If a system's structure and behavior is unknown or only partly known, it is impossible to predict failures due to cyber variation. (It may require major efforts even if all aspects are understood and documented.)

The principal cause of the 2003 East Coast power blackout, which left more than 50 million people without electricity, was determined by the U.S./Canada Power System Outage Task Force to be inadequate system understanding. A malfunctioning control system which was believed to be operational added to the sequence of events. As the report states, computer failures leading to loss of situational awareness in the control room, combined with the simultaneous loss of key transmission lines due to contact with trees, were the most important causes of the blackout. Thus, in this case, overgrown trees and a stormy night were the random outside variation, which would not have caused damage with a better degree of system understanding.

A lightweight system model, ideally documented as a set of diagrams that are supported by a configuration management database (CMDB), is essential for system understanding. It cannot be replaced by heavy verbal documentation which might be available as part of the system specification, because few people have the motivation, time, and education to digest and understand such documentation—which may hide relevant information scattered over hundreds or thousands of pages.

4.1   System Model Aspects and Criteria

A system model can serve different purposes. It can be used as a part of system design and specification, describing the SUC as it *should be*, and it can be used as part of system documentation, describing the SUC as it is.

A model is an abstracted description of the SUC, stripped down to the essentials that are necessary for system understanding. The goal is to produce the absolute essential minimum of documentation that makes it possible to understand the system—even by someone without on-site experience. In our case, two types of model span different areas, some of which are trivial, others of which can become quite complicated:

1. A *structural system model* breaks the IACS under consideration into smaller parts, and identifies the interactions among subsystems and interfaces to other systems.

2. An *execution environment* describes the cyber processes that are involved, including logical, physical, and organizational constraints.

Figure 4-1 illustrates the different aspects of a system model as a UML package diagram.

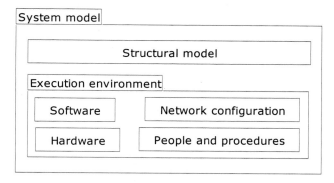

Figure 4-1   UML package diagram of a system model.

System model criteria in Figure 4-1 are that:

- A documented system model exists.
- The system model is stripped down to the minimum.
- The system model is verifiable.
- The system model is accurate.
- The system model is documented in a way that even uninvolved people without on-site experience (such as independent consultants, or co-workers from another department or another facility) are able to understand and verify the model.
- The system model is integrated with change management.

4.2   Building a Structural System Model

The recommended strategy to build a structural system model is top–down, starting with a model of the automated process and working down to cyber systems and processes that are involved in controlling the process. Modeling the system under consideration requires analytical effort.

Fragility observed: No structural model of the system under consideration exists. It is unclear which subsystems the SUC is composed of, what the interactions and dependencies among these subsystems are, and what interfaces to other systems exist.

Foundational requirement: To understand a system, its subsystems, dependencies, and interfaces to other systems must be known and documented.

> **Robustness target:** A model of the system under consideration exists that describes the system from a functional perspective and allows identification of all cyber subsystems and components that are required for functioning. System boundaries and interfaces are fully identified, from both a procedural/logistic and a cyber perspective.

Definition of Purpose, Scope, and Boundaries

A system model may serve different purposes. It may be constructed for planning, describing a nonexisting system that is about to be built. It may also be constructed to document the structure and functionality of an existing system. Last but not least, it is an interesting exercise for robustification to compare the model of an existing system with its original conceptual model; differences may point to system characteristics that have "grown" over several years of usage and may now jeopardize the reliability and maintainability of the system.

In a functional and process-oriented view, the system under consideration is never self-contained. It interfaces with other systems and processes. The boundaries of the system under consideration must be clearly identified in a system model. Such interfaces or boundaries exist in three independent areas, as illustrated below.

1. **Process logistics (supply chain):** The model may be for a large factory, for a specific assembly line, or for one specific machine or subprocess. The first task is to define the range of the landscape that is to be charted. Is it a town, a county, or a state? What is the geographic extent of the system under consideration? Depending on the desired granularity, the system under consideration may be deliberately limited to a specific plant, or to a specific machine or reactor, or even to specific automation components and field devices. The latter is the strategy of choice when defining procurement standards. For linear production processes, there are two natural process boundaries: Input of raw material, and output of product. A more complete model may be constructed by modeling several layers of granularity, ideally with the option to drill down into more detail if required.

2. **Network boundaries:** When modeling larger units, it is often the case that network traffic crosses domains, network segments, or zones. For example, there may be communication with systems and processes

located in the office (corporate) network, with systems located in other corporate facilities, or with systems located at vendors and contractors. Usually it is a good idea not to incorporate such networks, segments, or zones in the model, as it would get too complex.

3. **Noncyber boundaries:** Noncyber boundaries are interfaces from cyber to noncyber, for example,

   • Physical signal processing (sensors and actuators)

   • Human interfaces (displays and keyboards)

   • Additional I/O devices (scanners and printers)

What happens on the noncyber side of such interfaces—for example, the handling of printouts—is outside the scope of the system model.

Modeling a Physical Process

Building a structural model of a physical process usually is not a big deal. Most process engineers will be able to draw a diagram from scratch on the next napkin available. For example, a diagram for a simple three-step production process might look like Figure 4-2, where A, B, and C might represent subprocesses such as welding, painting, cutting, boiling, stirring, packaging, etc.

Figure 4-2   Example production process.

Unfortunately, a diagram like this lacks detail. How does material travel from A to B? How does it get to A in the first place? What other automated functions are required to run the subprocesses A, B, and C? Figure 4-2 shows only the process of stepwise adding value to material, hiding vital support systems that are also often automated, and that contribute importantly to the reliability or unreliability of the process. Figure 4-3 lists the various automated subsystems that are usually required in addition to processors in order to arrive at a sellable good. Table 4-1 provides brief descriptions of the subsytems in Figure 4-3.

Put together in a UML object diagram, it is now possible to draw a more detailed diagram of the simple ABC production process shown above, as in Figure 4-4.

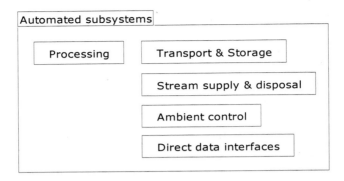

Figure 4-3   Example production process subsytems.

In Figure 4-4 it is assumed that the transport from processor B to processor C is done manually. Processors A and B require vacuum and emit exhaust gas that must be filtered. Processors B and C emit wastewater that must be cleaned. Finally, the area around processor C and transport T2 (which may include automated storage) must be cooled to maintain the product's quality. A quality inspection takes place between processor B and processor C, and a label printer is utilized to label the resulting product.

It should be evident that this diagram provides for a better starting point to model the controlling cyber systems than the simple three-step arrow model. When drawing diagrams like this, it is recommended to use different dimensions for material flow and supply/disposal streams, and different colors for the different classes of objects.

Modeling a Cyber Process

Cyber processes interact with each other via cyber interfaces. A cyber object does not have an interface to a physical process control object, but is linked to such objects via a dependency relation. An example UML package diagram is used in Figure 4-5 to illustrate the various software process categories that are usually found here.

The relationships shown in Figure 4-5 by dashed arrows can be read like this:

- The (automated) physical process is dependent on its controlling cyber processes.
- All cyber processes and interfaces are dependent on their *execution environment,* which has a logical, a physical, and an organizational

Table 4-1   Brief Descriptions of the Subcategories in Figure 4-3

Processors	Processors are the most obvious structure elements. They may be machines or assembly stations (in discrete manufacturing) or reactors (in process industries) that add value to material in order to ultimately form a product. Packaging machines are another example of processors.
Product transport and storage	Most automated physical production processes are not just about material manipulation. Where transport and storage is automated, it should be included in the model. For a complex production process, such as manufacturing automobiles, materials (body parts, for example) may travel several miles without leaving the plant. They don't do so on their own. Reliability problems in materials logistics have results very similar to processor unreliability.
Stream supply and disposal	Stream supply of vacuum, air pressure, ice, water, lubricants, etc., is vital for many processes, as is the disposal of scrap, wastewater, exhaust gases, etc. Where the respective aggregates are automated, they should be included in the model because they affect the reliability of the overall process. Many times, such systems are high priority because they serve multiple processors in the plant, so that downtime of an unsuspicious supportive system may easily result in plantwide downtime.
Ambient control	Ambient control systems, such as HVAC, may be required for production, transport, or storage of product (e.g., clean-room processes, processing/ transporting/storing fresh or frozen food). Where they are automated, they should also be entered into the model. Ambient control systems are special in that they usually don't connect to any of the other systems.
Direct data interfaces	Similar to logistics execution, direct data interfaces don't manipulate the product's properties, but they do collect or emit vital data about the product or the process. Examples are OEE counters (e.g., implemented with light barriers), MES lot label printers, or quality inspection sensors, which may even be integrated with transport, as in the case of in-line quality control.

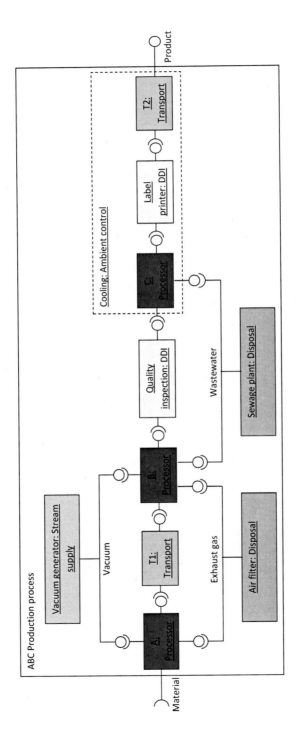

Figure 4-4 UML diagram for example ABC production process.

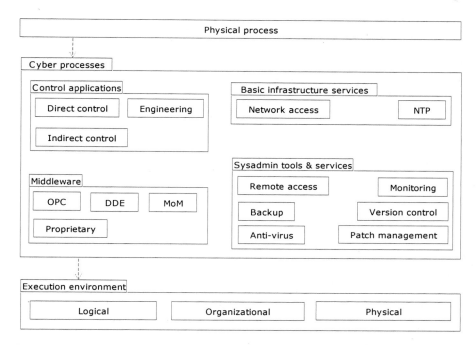

Figure 4-5 Example UML package diagram for cyber processes and execution environment.

part. The logical execution environment has attributes such as firmware, operating system, container version (JRE, Web browser, etc.), network address space, and access control lists. The physical execution environment has attributes such as processing speed, storage capacity, and quality of service (QoS). The organizational execution environment has attributes such as responsibility, standard operating procedures (SOPs), and service-level agreements (SLA).

The various categories in the cyber processes package are explained below.

- **Control applications:** Control applications can be grouped into three categories:

  1. *Direct control:* Applications that control (or at least visualize) a synchronous, physical process in real time. Examples are DCS and SCADA systems, and programs running on PLCs or controllers.

  2. *Indirect control:* Applications that control asynchronous, logical (as opposed to physical) processes without real-time constraints—

emergent processes that superimpose on the underlying synchronous process. Well-known examples include:

- Quality. Contemporary quality applications cover a wide range, from in-line quality inspections with automated scrap disposal to statistical process control (SPC). While such applications usually are not involved in physical process control (hence they are indirect), they may still be required to produce salable product. Examples are quality data for goods when product quality documentation is mandatory, such as in the pharmaceutical, automotive, and aircraft industries.

- Efficiency applications, or OEE, if not integrated with SCADA.

- Manufacturing execution systems, or MES, that link the production process with a business process. Common uses are pushing lot data into direct control applications, based on advanced scheduling algorithms and order/recipe databases.

Indirect control may interface with direct control applications (tier 2) or the process/product itself (tier 1), which will be discussed further below.

3. *Engineering tools:* that is, development and configuration applications, for the above-mentioned applications. As the term implies, such tools are usually used by engineers with domain expertise, rather than by IT specialists.

- **Basic infrastructure services:** These services provide information and resources that many systems and applications need even to start up, for example, network access and authentication. These services usually run autonomously and without user intervention. Most of them are linked to systems rather than to applications. Examples include:

  - Network access: DHCP, DNS

  - Domain access (Active Directory, RADIUS, etc.)

  - Network time protocol (NTP)

- **System administration and management tools & services:** Cyber processes in this category are intended to increase the overall reliability of a system. They allow administrators and maintenance engineers to perform housekeeping and diagnostic tasks. Examples include:

  - Remote access (RDP, VNC, PCAnywhere, etc.)

  - Monitoring (e.g., SNMP, Nagios)

- Backup servers

- Version control systems

- Antivirus solutions

- WSUS and similar proprietary software patch deployment services

• **Middleware:** OPC or DDE servers and message-oriented middleware (e.g., JMS), connect software processes in a (more or less) standardized, interoperable manner. Middleware runs autonomously, without user intervention, and is linked to applications.

Putting It All Together: Riveting Example

As has been noted, a structural model isn't worth much if it can't be visualized graphically. To do this, the Unified Modeling Language can be used. Figure 4-6 shows a diagram for a riveting control system and its associated subsystems and services. Network infrastructure interfaces (DHCP, DNS, AD) are shown as ports only. The riveting robot has an association with the physical riveting process, because the process is directly dependent on the robot's action. Quality inspection is integrated with control. A barcode reader, which delivers product identification to the riveting control PLC via a network interface, does not support DHCP but uses a static IP address, just like the PLC itself.

In Figure 4-6, interfaces that are used to exchange data required for the live controlled process are shown with solid (filled) ball diagrams, whereas interfaces which are asynchronous to the controlled process, such as a backup of quality data files, are displayed with open ball symbols. If any of the solid-ball interfaces go down, the process is forced to stop; if any of the open-ball interfaces get unavailable, this is not likely to have an immediate impact on the process. For example, being unable to generate backups will hardly stop the process.

It should be noted that the various boxes, or classes, in Figure 4-6 do not necessarily refer to physical systems (hardware platforms). For example, if the riveting control system talks to the robot through an OPC server, the OPC server should be modeled as a separate system, even if it is hosted on the same computer as the riveting control system. Also note that the boxes do not refer to specific software products, which are considered artifacts in UML terminology. Rather, the boxes refer to abstract cyber processes that process, transport, and store data.

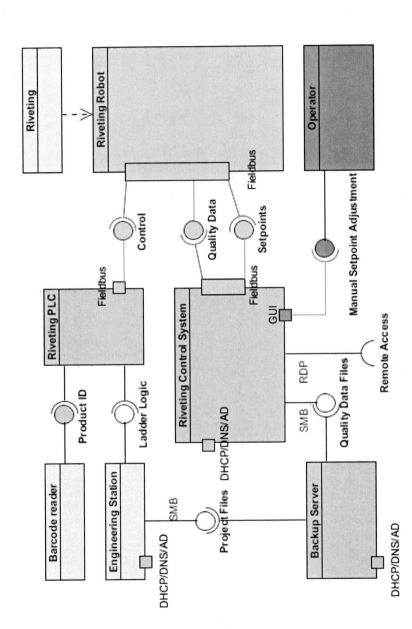

Figure 4-6 UML diagram for a riveting control system.

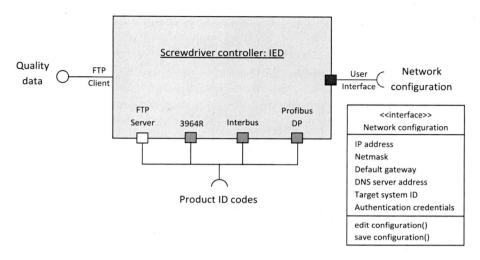

Figure 4-7   UML diagram for a screwdriver control system.

Modeling Isolated Systems: Screwdriver Example

The approach described here may also be applied to model systems in isolation, such as automation peripherals, to understand their interfaces and communication requirements. Figure 4-7 shows how an automated screwdriver with an Ethernet interface and various data links (two fieldbuses, one proprietary point-to-point) can be modeled.

In the Figure 4-7 example, the product features interfaces to accept product ID codes via FTP and three additional media. Product ID codes are internally paired with quality data, such as torque values. The consolidated quality data are provided by an FTP client interface.

The example also shows how to provide details for a specific interface. For the network configuration interface, it is shown which attributes are supplied via this interface, and that the interface provides two functions to edit and save configuration data.

Documenting the Execution Environment

Cyber processes are virtual. As such, they cannot exist on their own but are dependent on an execution environment, which can be split into logical, physical, and organizational parts. In the highway construction example in Chapter 3, the execution environment includes items such as topology (hills, rivers, swamps, etc.) and predominant weather conditions (temperature, precipitation, etc.). The next sections suggest methods for collecting information about the environment. As will be shown, most of these methods don't require an analytic process because items of the environment may be collected and described an in atomic manner. Ideally, items of the execution environment are linked to cyber processes. Usually this requires a CMDB system.

4.3   Hardware Inventory

A hardware inventory lists physical cyber systems that are required for the automated production process that is the scope of the robustness effort. In this context, *physical cyber system* means the hardware for data processing, transmission, or storage, including boundary devices such as printers and scanners.

Fragility observed: A hardware inventory of the system under consideration does not exist. It is undetermined which physical subsystems the system under consideration is comprised of and which other systems may interfere with the system's operation.

Foundational requirement: If the physical systems that are used to execute the specified cyber functions cannot clearly be identified, the system under consideration cannot be robustified.

Robustness target: A hardware inventory exists that can be verified against the real installation. The hardware inventory has entries for all physical systems and components that are covered by the scope of the specification. All entries are up to date and complete to the extent possible. The system inventory is accessible online by all authorized staff who must use inventory information. The system inventory is integrated with change management.

The hardware inventory should include all cyber systems that can affect automated process execution. Figure 4-8 shows possible classes of cyber hardware systems and is intended as an aid in collecting inventory information.

It should be noted that cyber is not limited to networked systems. A standalone system with no network interface may still be subject to robustification in its cyber aspects as long as it processes and stores data. For example, issues

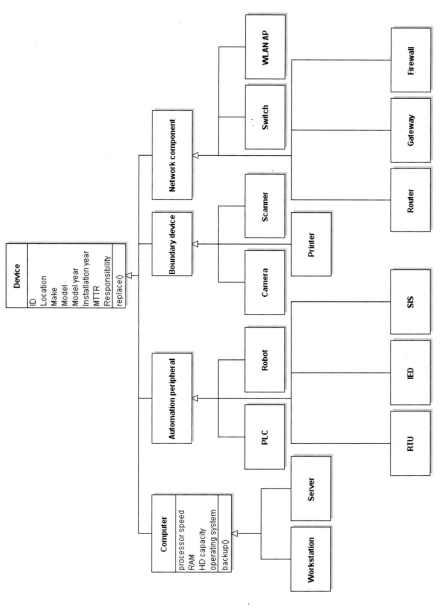

Figure 4-8 UML diagram for a hardware inventory.

such as user access policies, redundancy requirements, backup/restore, and change management all apply to non-networked systems. Therefore, non-networked systems should be included in the inventory.

For anything but the most simple installation, implementation of a hardware inventory requires a database that is integrated with change management. Many organizations still store hardware inventory information in spreadsheet tables, but this practice should be considered obsolete and inefficient.

4.4   Software Inventory

A software inventory contains details about the actual implementation of abstract cyber processes that were introduced in the section on structural modeling.

Fragility observed: An applications and services listing of the system under consideration does not exist. It is unclear which applications and services must run for the system to function. It is also unclear which applications and services do run on the system under consideration, even if perhaps they are not required.

Foundational requirement: Applications and services are the software and protocol implementation of specified functionality. They must be documented in order to assess robustness.

Robustness target: The application and services inventory specifies all applications and services that are required to perform the specified functionality of the system under consideration. All applications and services are cross-referenced to the hardware systems on which they are hosted. For all distributed applications and services, the technical details of data flow are specified. The application and services listing is integrated with change management.

In UML terminology, a software inventory may be thought of as the artifacts of abstract systems and processes. Figure 4-9 may be used as an aid to arrive at a software process repository.

Note: For anything but the most simple system, a database is required that is linked to the hardware inventory and to change management.

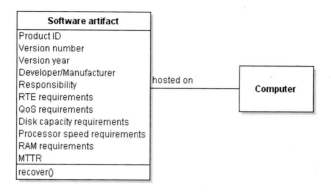

Figure 4-9   UML diagram for a software inventory.

4.5   Network Configuration

Network diagrams are nothing new or specific to industrial automation and control. They are required for determining the network traffic that is *technically possible*, along with essential transport characteristics such as quality of service (QoS), or bandwidth constraints (such as 10-Mbps half-duplex). Whereas network component hardware should be detailed in the hardware repository on an atomar level, a network diagram is required to understand network structure.

Fragility observed: Network architecture of the system under consideration is undocumented, or the documentation is out of date and inaccurate.

Foundational requirement: Where the system under consideration includes a network or multiple networks, the details of this network(s) must be documented, as technically possible network traffic and accessibility constitutes a major factor of a system's environment, or its components. Network architecture determines possible data flow, and thus possible interference.

Robustness target: A network architecture document exists that details the network architecture, endpoint systems, segmentation and zoning, firewalls, gateways, and interfaces to other networks. The network architecture document allows for identifying technically possible traffic from and to endpoint systems, access points, gateways, and interfaces. The network architecture document allows for determining the bandwidth, latency, and QoS characteristics of possible communication paths. The network architecture document is integrated into the change management process and is verified regularly.

Besides identifying the physical structure of a network, the following configuration information is equally important:

- Zoning: logical IP network layout, subnets, and routers; firewall rulesets and access control lists; VLAN segmentation; interfaces to other networks (office IT, peer PCNs, remote WAN access)
- Non-IP networks (e.g., Sinec H1, OSI), if present
- Fieldbus and point-to-point gateways
- WLAN access points, devices, and procedures

4.6   People, Policy, Procedures

Even a fully automated IACS installation requires people who interact with the system in one way or another. When assessing the fragility or robustness of IACS, it is essential to have a realistic understanding of who is responsible for what.

Fragility observed: People interacting with the system under consideration are not identified and have not been assigned to roles, groups, policies, and documented procedures. The system under consideration is accessible by unidentified individuals who may perform tasks to their preference.

Foundational requirement: Human users interacting with the system under consideration are an important aspect of the system's environment. If users, administrators, and their particular roles in interacting with the system are not specified, robustification is hardly possible.

Robustness target: Individuals who must or may interact with the system under consideration and its components are documented, along with responsibilities and duties. Responsibilities are specified using a role-based concept that is assignable to user groups. Repetitive tasks are formalized as standard operating procedures. The people and policies document lists the requirements for education and time allocation that must be met to fulfill the specified duties appropriately. All individuals who interact with the SUC are identifiable by name, department, and company (in the case of vendors and contractors). Procedures are documented and verifiable. The people and procedures document (or database) is integrated with the change management process.

The biggest challenge for PPP discipline is the commissioning phase. It is common that during this phase, an "anything goes" policy is assumed, where integrators and contractors may do almost anything they want in terms of cyber operations, usually with the goal of saving time (which may be another way to say: To get around poor planning).

Roles and Responsibilities

A basic approach to document and structure human interaction with cyber systems is to specify responsibilities and authorization. Usually this is a central part of cyber security policies.

It is suggested to use a functional view of human interactions that groups people according to their tasks that are to be performed with or applied to the system under consideration or its components. Sample task categories are operation, maintenance, safety, quality, business process interfaces optimization (MES, OEE), plant planning and procurement, and other (e.g., janitors). This part of the system model documents *who* is responsible for *what*. It may be expressed as a UML use case model, as in Figure 4-10.

The listing in Figure 4-10 should be cross-referenced with a staff database and organizational chart that ideally includes HR identifications. Third parties (vendors, contractors) should be referenced by pointing to existing vendor listings and service-level agreements.

Verifiable Procedure Descriptions

Even where education is at a high level, it is not sufficient to assign duties to trained staff without detailing execution. To evaluate the appropriateness of task definition and execution, and the variance of task execution for identical tasks performed repetitively and/or by different individuals, it is necessary to document the *when* and *how* for major tasks performed by humans when

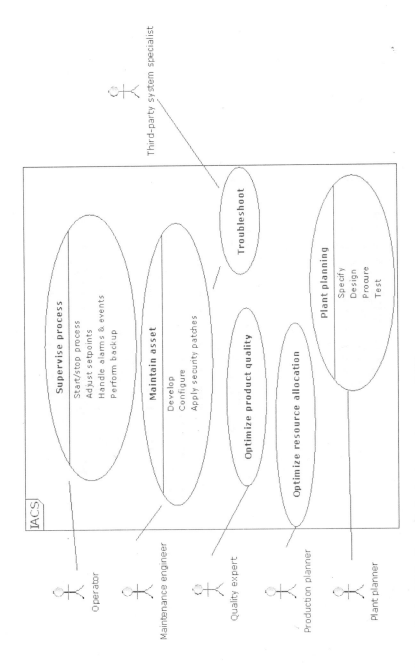

Figure 4-10 UML diagram for tasks and responsibilities.

dealing with IACS. Where it seems impossible to document the procedure as performed, or where it turns out that the same task is performed differently by different actors, this is an indication of fragility.

On real plant floors, detailed procedure descriptions are rarely part of policy but can be found in standard operation procedures (SOPs), if such SOPs exist for cyber-related procedures. Figure 4-11 illustrates how a procedure description for a backup process may be modeled using a UML activity diagram.

Since Stuxnet, SOPs have become much more important, especially in the form of contingency plans. The appropriate time to figure out how to cope with a significant malware hit is before it takes place, not after, when chaos may already have materialized and the whole organization is under tight time pressure. As the rule goes, a lousy plan today is better than a perfect plan tomorrow.

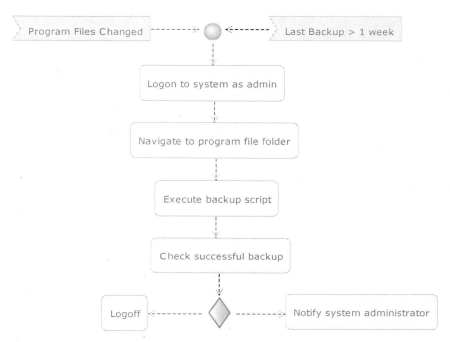

Figure 4-11 Example UML activity diagram for a backup process.

4.7   Monitoring and Auditing

Some characteristics of an IACS installation tend to change rather quickly. It is therefore not sufficient to build a system model for such characteristics and hope that they will remain as they are. System monitoring is a procedure for checking periodically to see whether said characteristics are still what they are supposed to be. The term *monitoring* is usually associated with technical system aspects; similar periodic checks applied to procedures are usually referred to as *auditing*.

Fragility observed: It is unknown whether actual cyber parameters and procedures are according to specification and policy, and within cyber operating limits; it may not even be known that some functions or subsystems are malfunctioning or already unavailable.

Robustification strategy: Monitoring cyber operating conditions for each subsystem so that conditions where such limits are reached can be prevented by human intervention. Auditing procedures allow for detection of deviation from policy, and thus for readjustment. Policies that are never, and probably even can't be, audited are worthless. Worthless policies are abundant on real plant floors; audits are an instrument to change them for the better.

Robustness target: Operators and maintenance staff have a clear and accurate picture of system status with respect to cyber operating limits. Procedures are performed according to policy.

Monitoring

Infrastructure monitoring is important in complex control system networks. It can be viewed as the dynamic complement of a system model. The system model tells about the system's static structure, but the only way to learn about the dynamic behavior of the system —especially where contingency areas may be reached—is by monitoring. Monitoring tells about deviation of target values, assuming such target values exist. It has often puzzled the author to see operators and maintenance staff working with barely an idea about the resources they had left, or the configuration and program changes somebody might have made at critical controllers—even after having experienced cybertrips in the past. Infrastructure monitoring is an area where commercial off-the-shelf solutions from IT are readily available. It is fair to say that in this area, IT is at least a decade ahead of the plant floor.

Table 4-2 summarizes contemporary monitoring solutions are available for several different important control system areas.

Table 4-2   Control System Monitoring Solutions

Asset condition monitoring	The difference between condition monitoring and safeguards is that condition monitoring focuses on preventing material damage for an asset (such as a specific machine), while safeguards focus on preventing process aberrations which might be hazardous to human health.
Resource monitoring (binary and analog contingency layer)	Monitoring of network bandwidth, network latency, disk space, memory space, and processor usage may all help to prevent (analog) contingency situations that may arise from insufficient resources. (See Singer, 2010.) This is the field of well-known network management solutions, incorporating protocols and services such as SNMP, along with add-ons such as Netflow. The most basic infrastructure monitoring solutions provide information at the binary layer; they inform an administrator as to whether certain systems are available on the network. This may be achieved, for example, by issuing periodical "ping" commands (ICMP echo requests).
Network access and interaction monitoring (digital contingency layer and above)	Intrusion detection systems (IDS) may help to detect cyber deviation at the digital layer and above. An intrusion detection system may, for example, notify an administrator of data that is exfiltrated from the process network, or about a rogue system that is connected to the network (if such connection isn't already prevented by network port security).

Auditing

Auditing is similar to monitoring in the sense that it provides a reality check of the installation's properties. However, different from monitoring, auditing is usually associated with conformance. To establish conformance, a policy (or similar form of regulation) is required.

Auditing may affect technical characteristics and in some cases may be almost completely automated, such as when checking the patch level of all computers in a specific network segment. Other areas of auditing stretch to procedures, such as backup procedures performed by staff members, or access control procedures, and might require a walk-around. Audits that cannot be performed in an automated way are usually done at long intervals, such as every two years, to save the labor (and potential traveling) involved.

Chapter 5

Requirements and System Specification

System specification plays a vital role in robustification. Even more than a system model, meeting certain formal characteristics has a large influence on the value of a specification. A system specification is, for example, essential for reducing design variation. Similar to a policy, a specification may be so vague that many technically different possible system designs could still be specification conformant, resulting in unnecessary variation. What compliance is for policy, conformance is for specification.

System specification criteria are as follows:

- A system specification is available as a written document.
- Subject-matter experts are able to verify that the functionality, implementation, configuration, and execution procedures specified lead to a solution that fulfills the stated requirements.
- Applying the system specification produces a working solution.
- Application of the system specification by different people leads to identical results.
- Determinations by different people as to whether a given system design is specification conformant leads to identical results.
- The system specification is integrated with change management.

5.1   The Role of Requirements for Robustification

The application of robustification strategies changes a system. Such change is worthwhile only if the system's functionality isn't sacrificed, and if the new system characteristics—hopefully, better robustness among them—can be viewed as progress.

Robustification is an engineering discipline that teaches how to solve a technical problem better than before. This is only possible if a clear understanding of required functionality exists, something that is usually not part of a system model. While a good system model tells how a specific system is designed, it usually does not explain why this particular design was chosen. Being able to answer "why" questions is a major prerequisite for robustification. Being unable to identify the rationale for certain system design decisions, on the other hand, is an indication of incomplete system understanding.

Requirements are not subject to robustification efforts, and robustification makes no attempt to verify that documented requirements are appropriate. In actual robustification projects, this is an important topic to communicate to end users, who usually fear that their requirements will no longer be met after their system has been "improved" by third parties.

Table 5-1   Functional Specification Elements

	Specification Item	Example 1	Example 2
A	**Requirement**	Quick troubleshooting by system expert, who may not be on site	Availability of data, programs, etc.
B	**Function**	Remote access	Backup
C	**Implementation**	Dial-in modem, proprietary remote desktop product	Disk mirror image; SMB copy
D	**Configuration**	Specific modem product(s) and software product(s) to be used; authentication and encryption settings	Number and IP address(es) of backup server(s)
E	**Execution procedure**	Access granted after preceding telephone call from machine operator	Which files/directories, in which interval, automatic or manual; backup procedure of server

5.2   Specification Items

A functional specification links requirements, function, implementation, configuration, and execution procedure. These elements may be separated as shown in Table 5-1.

Separating the specification items in Table 5-1 allows for the opportunity to replace fragile implementations with robust implementations while still delivering required functionality. If this granularity is omitted, typical problems result.

- **Specification flaw #1: Specification ends prematurely downward.** This leaves room for variability, whereby different functions, implementations (products), or procedures (configurations) can be used that all are specification conformant.

  The requirement for quick troubleshooting is often fulfilled by remote access. It is left open, however, how remote access is to be implemented and executed. Consequently, in real installations, a mix of dial-in modems is used along with Internet/VPN access, using different protocols and products.

  A company in the automotive industry specifies that new installations use Profinet, leaving open the question of which Profinet variant (RT, RT/UDP, or IRT) must be used. The asset owner may see many different implementations in the future which still are all specification conformant.

- **Specification flaw #2: Specification ends prematurely upward.** This simply mandates a specific product, technology, or functionality, without telling why. Since requirements and functionality are not detailed, there is little opportunity to replace the mandated solution with an alternative, for example, if the product or technology in question becomes obsolete and is no longer available for purchase.

  A component vendor uses Remote Procedure Calls (RPC) as a method for client/server communication for its control system solution. It is pointed out that this protocol is an obstacle for robustification, if only because it uses dynamic TCP ports and thus prevents optimum use of firewalls. However, the vendor argues that using RPC is a requirement. The question of why the design decision for RPC had been made could not be answered.

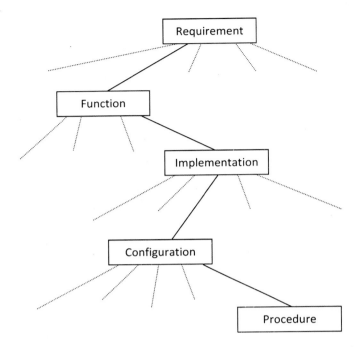

Figure 5-1 A specification tree. Requirements are at the root (top), and are not subject to robustification. The specification tree for a given system should extend down to procedures, so as to limit variability.

5.3 The Specification Tree

For any requirement, there is usually more than one way in which its function can be fulfilled. For any function, there is usually more than one way in which it can be implemented. And for any implementation, there is usually more than one way in which it can be executed in terms of configuration, environment, context, etc. Therefore, as shown in Figure 5-1, specification is similar to a decision tree, where each new branch opens up a new set of variability.

A good specification limits the number of possible functions, implementations, configurations, and procedures—ideally, to a single instance in every node, thereby reducing variability. A good specification doesn't allow for arbitrary alternative functions, implementations, and procedures. Ideally, there should only be one possible specification-conformant implementation—that is, only one specific path from requirement (root) to procedure (leaf). However, a good specification also allows for determining whether alternative procedures, implementations, and functions—which may be more robust than the original solution—still meet requirements. This is an essential foundation for robustification.

Robustification is a procedure for identifying and selecting alternate paths in the specification tree that limit variation while still fulfilling requirements. This aspect of robustification can be illustrated using Example 2 in Table 5-1. Shared folders are a common but fragile means of performing backups (see the discussion of antistructure attractors in Chapter 2). If this implementation is replaced with an alternative that limits variability, such as secure FTP (SFTP) or secure copy (SCP), fragility is reduced to a large extent without violating requirements. If it is done properly, end users and/or automated software processes will not even notice the difference.

It should also be clear by this point that any robustification effort will result in specification change that must be properly planned and documented.

5.4   Specifying Cyber Operating Conditions

Operating conditions specify the conditions under which a given implementation and/or procedure is tested and reliable, and under which it is not. For electrical characteristics such as power supply, this is standard for any contemporary system or product; for cyber, it is not.

Resource Requirements and Dependencies

Specification must identify all resources that must be supplied by the system's environment in order for the system to perform as specified. For example, if there is a need for

- A DHCP server, DNS server, or NTP server, accessible via the network
- A specific third-party product such as a database engine
- A specific software component such as a DLL in a specific version

to be present in order for the system to function, most likely with dedicated configuration settings, this must be documented.

Operating Limits: Conditions That Must Be Avoided for Proper Performance

Every technical system has operational limits beyond which functionality is impaired, and operating preconditions that must be met for the system to work. The designer and implementer of the system expect that the system will be operated within these limits. Unfortunately, this does not imply that such limits, which are as real as their electrical counterparts, are necessarily properly documented.

Cyber variation is not the same as invalid inputs, errors, stress, and faults. Errors and faults are violations of specified parameters. If no specification exists, it cannot be violated—yet real systems still do fail even in the absence of specification, due to de-facto violation of operating conditions (which exist physically, logically, and procedurally), which is not identical to de-jure violation of operating conditions as specified (if specified). A system without specified operating limits is fragile, because the performance of the system under given conditions cannot be predicted or guaranteed.

> *The documentation of a controller for automated screwdrivers with integrated FTP server specifies that FTP other than "put" are not supported and may cause problems. While this is obviously less than ideal, it is much better than leaving it open to the user's imagination what may happen if arbitrary commands are sent to the unit.*
>
> *An automation peripheral with a 10-Mbps network interface is incompatible with 100-Mbps auto-sensing network switches and fails randomly if it is attached to such network gear. However, this is not documented. It is experienced empirically by the end user, who invests many person-days to discover this "hidden" operating condition.*

The examples above illustrate operational limitation on the digital cyber contingency layer. However, operational limits should be specified for all cyber contingency layers. For example, on the analog layer, items such as required disk space, memory space, processing speed, and network latency are of interest.

Along with operating limits, specification should contain a definition of test cases that can be used to verify whether the SUC performs to specification.

Chapter 6

Imposing Structure

In most real-world IACS installations, many functional and accessibility options exist that are not required to fulfill the system's specified purpose and that don't add value to the system under consideration. Required functionality, accessibility, or variation in implementation, operation and maintenance is therefore a subset of what is actually installed. The additional options, or *delta*, that are not required provide for fragility without adding value. If this delta is reduced, ideally to zero, then robustness is increased without decreasing a system's value. Reduction strategies aim at stripping down variability as much as possible without reducing a system's ability to deliver required functionality. It's basically a "Do what is necessary, but not more" approach, which aims at providing bare necessities, but doing so in a very reliable manner. Certainly this is only possible if a clear understanding of such required functionality exists.

Reduction strategies can also be viewed as imposing structure on the respective installation. Reducing variability (and entropy) is almost identical to creating order. For example, a production network shows a higher degree of structure if automation peripherals can be accessed only by SCADA applications and engineering stations, and not by power-consumption meters, contractors' remote workstations, or barcode printers.

Reduction strategies can be applied very successfully in IACS environments because such environments tend to be much more static than office IT. The following areas include candidates for reduction strategies:

- **Functionality:** For static applications, there is no benefit in providing more functionality than is required. The principle of limiting transfer function range can be applied here and will result in a more robust system.

- **Accessibility:** There is no benefit in making a system accessible to more systems and users than is required. The principle of blocking invalid input can be applied here and will result in a more robust system.
- **Implementation and procedures:** There is no benefit in solving identical problems in different ways. The consistency principle can be applied here and will result in a more robust system.

Figure 6-1 shows the flexibility pizza. It is easy to see that the crust is very big. However, even crust lovers don't buy pizza just for the crust. The juicy stuff in the center is essential; if it's missing, or very small, the whole pizza won't be worth buying. For IACS, the same is true for functionality, accessibility, and variation in procedure. If the crust is cut away, requirements are still met, and the chance for cyber trips is diminished.

The following sections illustrate several best-practice approaches to reducing nonrequired functionality.

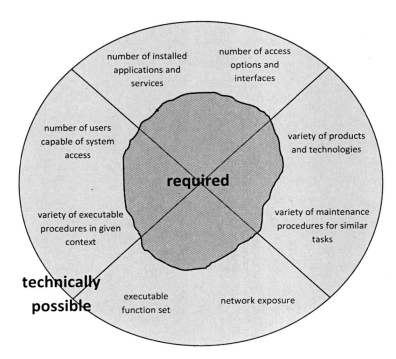

Figure 6-1   The flexibility pizza. Required functionality is a subset of installed functionality. This is what makes an installation flexible—and fragile.

6.1 Removing Unnecessary Applications, Services, and Functions (System Hardening)

Common wisdom among chemical safety engineers says, "What you don't have can't leak" (Kletz, 1978), meaning that by reducing the number of tanks in a plant, the number of potential problems is usually reduced too. The same holds true for cyber. It refers to what in IT security is known as *system hardening*.

Fragility observed: The system under consideration is populated with unnecessary applications and services, or it is unknown whether unnecessary applications and services are installed and activated on the system under consideration.

Robustification strategy: Unnecessary applications and services increase the probability of unauthorized system use, implementation flaws, and side effects (storage/CPU/network exhaustion) without offering any benefit. Removing or disabling such functions and services reduces the potential for undesired side effects.

Robustification principle: Limit transfer function range (system level).

Robustness target: The system under consideration is free from unnecessary applications and services, or such applications and services have been disabled.

Applications and services that are not installed on one's server can't crash or otherwise impair the system's primary (and often only) task. They can't consume resources (memory, CPU, disk), can't transmit data that's not required for the IACS functionality, can't be crashed by malware, etc., with the accompanying potential for side effects for the control application. Every software application, service, and interface, and the network connectivity associated with it, introduces a new degree of freedom to the system, and therefore adds potential for fragility. Practical problems associated with such nonrequired degrees of freedom include consumption of CPU power and memory, network bandwidth, waste of staff time, and potential implementation faults that may cause the host system to crash. Industrial automation and control systems serve a very limited, static purpose. There is no need, and usually no desire, to have a control system server host interactive games, personal productivity tools, media players, or office applications, even though such applications have been found on DCS and SCADA servers.

The problem gets even bigger if it is taken into account that many of such unnecessary applications may be automatically updated during the system's lifecycle, and may also trigger the installation of security patches that might affect the behavior of vital software processes. One of the most bizarre ways to cause control system malfunction is by installing security patches that are not required or helpful for central software processes but only for applications and services that have no business being on the system in the first place. This is equal to changing the execution environment.

> *The standard Microsoft Windows installation comes with not only media players and interactive games installed, but also with several network services enabled (such as DCOM, NetBIOS, SMB), which may not be required by the target application but present a significant potential for malfunction. In other words, using a standard Windows box without modification introduces fragility on the plant floor.*

Unfortunately, it has become common for vendors of automation peripherals to extend their products with nonessential cyber features such as Web servers. Because they are not really essential, such features are usually not tested as thoroughly as production functionality. Understanding that it is difficult (and costly) enough to implement robust core technology, it should be self-explanatory why it is a good idea to do without any nonessential gadgets.

A solution less radical than de-installation is to make applications and services configurable, so that the system administrator may chose to disable a specific functionality rather than uninstalling it.

> *Consider the following example as a reality check. An average Windows PC hosts several hundred thousand files. Do you know— as an administrator, maintenance engineer, or software developer— which applications, components, and services are required for a specific system and which are not? As a result of software complexity, many experts don't. This leads to systems that are populated with all kinds of nonrequired programs, DLLs, services, etc., among them perhaps malicious code. For example, Stuxnet renamed the legitimate driver DLL that it replaced to s7otbxsx.dll. This can be discovered easily. Would this DLL raise your suspicions if there is an application with the file name s7otbxsx.exe in the same folder?*

In real life, the hardest part of system hardening is not removing or disabling software applications and components, but determining which files are required and which are not. Doing this for existing systems without the help of the vendor leads to reverse engineering, which is time-consuming and costly. The best approach to system hardening is having the vendor deliver a hardened system at commissioning, along with extensive documentation.

Efforts toward system hardening— for both computers and controllers— can be guided by focusing on the following types of files particularly, with emphasis on determining whether the files are required for the intended purpose of the system under consideration.

- **Application programs:** The average computer system is populated with many application programs that serve no useful purpose for the intended operation. For example, many plant floor systems are equipped with games, Internet Relay Chat software, picture and document viewers, and office applications. Chances are that such undesired applications trigger multiple security patches during system lifetime.

- **Component software and "open" interfaces:** Application programs are not implemented in monolithic blocks. Instead, the average application makes use of several software components that are usually implemented as dynamic link libraries. Sometimes, such components may implement interfaces for third-party applications which may allow for significant manipulation of program and process behavior.

The SCADA application attacked by Stuxnet comes with an integrated OPC server by default (which was not exploited by Stuxnet). Many users of this product don't use the OPC server and don't even know that it exists. It can, however, be accessed by any OPC client, which may result in significant process manipulation.

Almost any modern SCADA or DCS product comes with proprietary interfaces for data exchange with third-party applications such as quality management or MES. More than once, such interfaces have been advertised as "open" connectivity options. Unfortunately, the concept of "open" usually also means unauthenticated.

- **Network services:** Identifying nonrequired network services is more difficult than locating undesired application programs, because such services don't have a user interface. They run silently in the background. The average computer user has no idea how to check which network services are running and what would happen if those services were disabled.

Consider this example as a reality check. On your Windows computer system, launch a command box by executing the program CMD after selecting the "execute program" menu item in the start menu. In the command box, execute "netstat −a". What you will see is a listing of network services running on your computer. Can you tell what exactly these services are doing, and whether they are required for the tasks you use your computer for?

Some of the more questionable network services can be found not only on computers but also on controllers and on automation peripherals such as RTUs and IEDs. Most prominently, these include HTTP, FTP, and SNMP servers.

Disabling nonrequired network services is the most effective step in system hardening, because such services provide for the highest potential of system output variability. For example, DCOM alone allows for reconfiguring a Windows computer via the network in almost any respect, including the removal and installation of system services, manipulations of the Windows registry, etc.

- **Nonexecutable files:** Many computer systems on the plant floor are cluttered with unnecessary nonexecutable files such as

  – Unneeded documentation
  – Obsolete configuration files
  – Spreadsheet and database files

These files might once have been created for development or testing purposes but have been left on the system for no good reason. Such files will usually enter into periodic backups. Years later, maintenance may have no idea whether they are required.

Robustification Procedure

Step 1. *Document what you have.* For the system under consideration, document the major application programs, software components, and network services that are installed and activated. The vendor may be a big help here. For new systems, a listing of required application programs, component software, and network services should be part of the system documentation supplied by the vendor.

Step 2. *Document what you need.* For the system under consideration, document which application programs, software components, and network services are needed, and why.

Step 3. *Identify and close the gaps.* Remove or disable as many unnecessary application programs, software components, and network services as practical. For new systems, this task should be performed by the vendor or integrator.

Step 4. *Document changes.* Update the system documentation to reflect the new system configuration.

Step 5. *Pursue consistency and sustainability.* Apply the changes consistently to identical or similar systems. Make sure that any new identical or similar system uses the stripped-down configuration from start. Make it a common policy that new systems are hardened by the vendor or integrator before commissioning.

6.2   Reducing or Removing General-Purpose Software Services and Interfaces

Anyone with a background in IT security has learned that the ability to execute arbitrary code, usually by exploiting buffer overflows, is bad. Funny enough, there are many more ways to execute arbitrary code and trigger a wide range of functionality than through exploiting buffer overflows, which are considered to be software defects. The easiest way to do this is to use software interfaces and services that are especially designed for this purpose, and that are not considered as "bugs" at all.

Fragility observed: The system under consideration hosts general-purpose services and application hooks that allow for arbitrary code execution, or it is unknown whether the system under consideration hosts general-purpose services and application hooks that allow for arbitrary code execution.

Robustification strategy: The functional extent of a software service as implemented should not be bigger than the functionality required. If a general-purpose software service can be replaced by a limited-purpose software client without loss of required functionality, the variation potential is reduced, and so is fragility.

Robustification principle: The blockout principle (limit transfer function range).

> **Robustness target:** The system under consideration does not host general-purpose services and application hooks which allow for arbitrary code execution.

Some software services offer much more functionality than others. In the name of flexibility and convenience, they are more powerful. But because they are so powerful, they are also often the target of malware. Prime examples on IT platforms are services that allow for code execution. Where such services and interfaces are activated, it can be difficult or impossible to limit the variation of output behavior. For example, simple parameter changes (intentional or accidental) may lead to vastly different output behavior. Sometimes, such powerful and flexible interfaces are used mainly because they provide simple connectivity without much planning in advance—that's why we referred to them previously as *antistructure attractors*. The downside is that where more functionality than required is technically possible, chances are that it will actually be used at some point—either as part of a quick-and-dirty workaround, or accidentally, or even maliciously. No matter what the reason may be, experience regularly shows that the de-facto use of general-purpose software services exceeds by far what the operator or planner had intended.

Reducing or removing general-purpose software applications and services may be viewed as a strategy similar to system hardening, where the hardening is executed on a functional level per application or service, rather than on a system level. In situations where the interfaces in question cannot be disabled for practical reasons, emphasis should be put on reducing the accessibility of such interfaces by means of network zoning and authentication (combinatorial leverage of robustification efforts). Some areas to focus on include the following.

- **General-purpose network services:** Some network services on a Windows system are so powerful that they allow for a complete reconfiguration of the system. Others are not as powerful, but still open up the potential for introducing changes that may adversely impact the behavior of critical applications. The major services that should be examined in a robustification project are

  - RPC (Remote Procedure Calls)

  - DCOM (Distributed Component Object Model)

  - SOAP (Simple Object Access Protocol)

  - RDP (Remote Desktop Protocol)

Network services such as RPC and DCOM can often be replaced by application-specific client/server protocols that reduce output variability significantly. Certainly this requires cooperation from the vendor. When using RDP, emphasis should be placed on restricting access.

Stuxnet exploited RPC for its peer-to-peer update functionality.

- **Local and network command shells:** The ability to open the local command window (CMD) on Windows systems has led to numerous problems on engineering and operation systems, especially in conjunction with transportable media. The counterparts of the CMD window are network command shells such as *Telnet* and *Rlogin*. While they can hardly be used in conjunction with transportable media, they certainly can be used to reconfigure the target system to a point that it is no longer capable of fulfilling its designated purpose in a control system environment.

- **The auto-run configuration setting:** Configuring a Windows system for auto-run of applications on transportable media may sooner or later lead to the execution of applications which may have a negative impact on the legitimate applications the system hosts. One of the worst aspects of auto-run is the fact that the applications launched from transportable media are usually unknown to the operator, leading to unpredictable system behavior.

Stuxnet exploited a bug in the Windows operating system that allowed for execution of arbitrary code on transportable media. While this bug, known as the LNK vulnerability, has been fixed by Microsoft, the auto-run configuration setting has not, because it is not considered a bug. Any system with auto-run activated is as prone to execution of arbitrary code on transportable media as a system with no patch for the LNK exploit.

- **Application-specific hooks for program execution:** Some applications have scripting capabilities or even go so far to provide shell interfaces that allow for the execution of arbitrary binary code, such as command shell interfaces or DLL interfaces that are called automatically. In essence, this may result in a semi-auto-run functionality. Different from the auto-run of the operating system, chances are that application-specific hooks cannot be disabled by the end user.

> *Stuxnet exploited an application-specific, undocumented ability of the PLC programming application to execute program code that is located in the project folder.*

Another example for this category is the opportunity to execute arbitrary function calls from database tables (SQL injection). This may be particularly concerning if the application in question is executed with powerful credentials, such as administrator rights.

> *Stuxnet exploited stored procedure calls in the database of the affected SCADA product.*

Robustification Procedure

Step 1. *Document what you have.* For the system under consideration, document the existing general-purpose interfaces and services that are installed, activated, and used. The vendor or integrator may be a big help here.

Step 2. *Document what you need.* For the system under consideration, document which interfaces and services are actually required, and why.

Step 3. *Identify and close the gaps.* Determine whether the required functionality can as well be provided by application-specific interfaces. Replace as many general-purpose interfaces and services with application-specific interfaces and services as practical.

Step 4. *Document changes.* Update the system documentation to reflect the new system configuration.

Step 5. *Pursue consistency and sustainability.* Make sure that any new identical or similar system uses the stripped-down configuration. Update procurement guidelines to reflect the restricted system configuration.

6.3   Using Application-Specific Least-Functionality Interfaces

Modern controllers require different types of interactions with their IT environment. For example, a major distinction can be made between the interaction with an engineering station (used for development and configuration) and with a SCADA system (used for display and manipulation of process variables). If there is the technical opportunity that an HMI station, for example, can reconfigure a controller that it only needs to probe for process value changes, this functionality may at some point actually be used, and not necessarily in the best interest of the asset owner.

Fragility observed: The system under consideration offers general-purpose interfaces that are used by multiple applications for different purposes, with some applications using only a fraction of functionality compared to what is technically possible. The system under consideration is also considered fragile if it is unknown whether general-purpose interfaces are provided.

Robustification strategy: Providing least-functionality interfaces for different application types (use cases).

Robustification principle: The blockout principle (limit input variability).

Robustness target: The system under consideration offers different interfaces for different application types with least functionality, or supports authentication/authorization to limit application types to least functionality. A system of a specific application type does not have the opportunity to interact with the system under consideration in a manner that would be used by another application type.

In the case of Stuxnet, the attacked controller products feature one very powerful application protocol that essentially allows the connected system to execute every function on the controller—from reading process values to complete reconfiguration. Computer access to this protocol is implemented in a driver DLL that exports the complete range of functionality to any client application. This driver DLL is used both by the vendor's engineering software and by its SCADA product. By hijacking the driver DLL, Stuxnet was capable of changing controller configuration even on systems that were running only the SCADA application, without the engineering application.

There is not a great variety of different IT application types in modern IACS environments, and history tells us that a new application type occurs only about once per decade. If these application types use application-specific interfaces, chances for random, accidental, or malicious function escalation is minimized. A good starting point would be to provide different interfaces for engineering and SCADA applications. Where this is not the case, one can expect that the most powerful interface is used, which is usually the engineering interface. Thus, any counterpart connected to the system in question may have many more opportunities to manipulate the system's behavior (not necessarily intentionally) than what is required.

In a nutshell, limiting the functionality of interfaces to what is needed for a specific application is similar to the concept of role-based authorization from IT security, with the major difference that here it is not about restricting the capabilities of human users but those of specific applications. Therefore, an alternative to using different technical protocols for such different interfaces (also known as *port partitioning*) is the implementation of authentication and authorization logic that enables the target system to restrict accessible functionality per client, based on authorization templates. Areas to focus on include the following.

- **Engineering interfaces:** Engineering interfaces are used for development of control logic and for and controller reconfiguration. They are usually not limited to the capability of loading code and configuration data on peripherals. For testing and debugging purposes, they may also have the capability to monitor program execution and process variables. In essence, an engineering interface usually provides "all" functionality that the respective product has to offer. Access should therefore be restricted to those few systems (i.e., engineering stations) that actually need such unlimited functionality.

- **Interfaces for user applications (SCADA, quality control, MES):** Interfaces for user applications are mostly about the capability to monitor and manipulate process variables such as temperatures, pressures, recipe component amounts, lot quantities, etc. It is not desired for an operator or a quality manager to change process logic.

- **Intercontroller communication:** Controllers may exchange information with peer controllers such as product ID, serial number, and quality data. A sample use case is material flow management. Required functionality is usually only a subset of SCADA interaction, and may feature some special requirements such as message-based communication.

- **Asset and function monitoring:** Modern intelligent peripherals offer several capabilities to monitor system health and status. The general product trend clearly is to make automation peripherals as intelligent as possible, and to make that intelligence network accessible.

Robustification Procedure

Step 1. *Document what you have.* For the system under consideration, document the existing interfaces to IT applications and peer peripherals. The vendor or integrator may help.

Step 2. *Document what you need.* For the system under consideration, document the type of functionality that such applications actually require.

Step 3. *Identify and close the gaps.* Replace as many general-purpose interfaces with least-functionality application-specific interfaces as practical. Usually this can only be done by the vendor.

Step 4. *Document changes.* Document the new system configuration.

Step 5. *Pursue consistency and sustainability.* Similar products from other vendors also use application-specific interfaces or restrict interface functionality by authentication and authorization.

6.4   Reducing Static Open File Exchanges (Shared Folders)

The standard file system is culturally established as a central paradigm for information exchange in the automation and control space. Engineers tend to use this paradigm almost intuitively. Not only can information that is stored in files be copied to transportable media, it can also be structured in a simple way (by using folders), and the structure can be viewed and modified easily by using ubiquitous software applications such as Windows Explorer.

Fragility observed: The system under consideration offers static open file exchanges that allow users to exchange files between different systems, without the necessity to delete transferred files after copying, and without enforcing strict ownership and version control. The system under consideration is also considered fragile if it is unknown whether static open file exchanges are provided.

Robustification strategy: Reducing the number of files on a system that nobody knows what purpose they have but everybody is afraid to delete because of unknown side effects.

Robustification principle: The avoid-mess principle.

Robustness target: The system under consideration does not offer static open file exchanges. Files that need to be exchanged with other systems are copied by secure, transactional procedures.

Exchanging files among different systems is a necessity in real-world control system environments. Such files may be configuration and program files that need to be copied to other systems, data files for backup, or spreadsheet tables and documents that engineers want to copy to their personal notebook computers. However, few people who use shared folders take the effort to delete files that are no longer needed on that particular computer system (for example, after having been copied to another system, or to a thumb drive), and even fewer people dare to delete files from other users that cannot be associated with any given legitimate application program. Several months later, nobody can tell the exact purpose of every file in a shared folder. When looking at the contents of any shared folder, questions such as: Is this file required? Who owns this file? What will happen if I delete this file? often cannot be answered. And since it is unknown whether all these files are needed, they are sometimes treated as essential configuration files that go into every backup. That's the simple reason why shared folders are referred to as *antistructure attractors*. They tend to produce chaos.

> *It should be no surprise that Stuxnet used shared folders as a means of spreading inside an infected LAN environment. Shared folders are so common in real-world control system networks that it was just natural for Stuxnet to exploit them. The benefit for any malware is that shared folders not only help in spreading from one system to other systems, they are also a good place to hide, since users and administrators often don't have any idea what the purpose of files in a shared folder might be, and leave them alone for just this reason—an example of the "never touch a running system" syndrome (see the Appendix).*

The major file sharing services in use today are

- SMB/CIFS
- NFS

Shared folders are called *static* here because they are not transaction-based. The file stays there after it is copied to its destination. It must be deleted manually. Often, it isn't. Shared folders are popular not because of functionality, but because of convenience. Functionality can be provided as well by transactional services. Another, nontechnical solution is to enforce the policy that shared folders are purged regularly every week or every month.

Robustification Procedure

Step 1. *Document what you have.* For the system under consideration, document the existing shared folders and their use.

Step 2. *Document what you need.* For the system under consideration, document what the information exchange done via shared folders is actually needed for.

Step 3. *Identify and close the gaps.* Replace as many shared-folder operations as possible with transactional protocols, and/or enforce purge policies.

Step 4. *Document changes.* Document the new system configuration.

Step 5. *Pursue consistency and sustainability.* Shared folders are an issue for *all* IT systems. Try to remove shared folders from as many systems as possible, and make sure that new systems are configured without shared folders. Try to prevent procuring or developing IT applications that mandate the use of shared folders.

6.5   Eliminating Hidden Hubs

A hidden hub is a computer system or file system that is often thought of as a trusted endpoint, but it really isn't one. Prime examples are engineering notebooks that are used for local access to sensible systems and then travel to other sites, and computer systems that are connected to sensible systems via modem or Internet VPN connection for remote maintenance. If that same computer system is used to surf the Web or to connect to other (more or less) sensitive systems in different networks—for example, from different clients in the case of contractors—what was thought of as an endpoint may become a hub that can be used – knowingly or not—to exchange information and files with other systems.

Fragility observed: The system under consideration is network accessible by agents that may link to nontrusted and unknown systems in uncontrolled ways. The system under consideration is also considered fragile if it is unknown whether hidden hubs exist.

> **Robustification strategy:** Making sure that third-party access to the system under consideration terminates at a known and trusted third-party system.
>
> **Robustification principle:** Blocking invalid input (from technical systems).
>
> **Robustness target:** There are no uncontrolled access points to the system under consideration. From controlled access points, no uncontrolled traffic to other systems is possible.

Compared to a hidden hub, a static open file exchange (see above) has the advantage that it is visible, including all the files that it contains, even if few people can make sense out of all those file names. A hidden hub, on the other hand, is invisible to local administrators, yet has the same (or even worse) drawbacks. *Hidden hubs* are file exchanges that are invisible and remote, i.e., not under the control of local administrators. Their sheer existence may even be unknown.

If there is one thing that should concern every asset owner with respect to Stuxnet, it's the malware's geographic distribution. While it is clear that Stuxnet was meant to attack certain systems in Iran that couldn't be targeted directly by the attackers, we see infected systems even in Europe and in the United States—this in respect to a malware that was specifically designed not to spread as widely as possible. In technical terms, Stuxnet is more a virus than a worm: It relies mainly on thumb drives and shared folders for spreading.The explanation for Stuxnet's distribution as it manifest is easy; it's just like back in the old days of computer viruses.

Structurally, hidden hubs work similarly to the "small world experiment" that was originally designed by psychologist Stanley Milgram. Milgram was one of the first to discover that any person can reach virtually any other person in the world using very few intermediate social interactions via overlapping social networks. This model can also be applied to malware distribution which exploits procedures designed for "local" interaction, i.e., without using the capabilities of the Internet for global mass distribution. Many different contractors may access infected systems (via shared folders, shared printers, and thumb drives), and most of these contractors serve other clients. Some of these other clients may be located in different countries, perhaps even on different continents. Some of these other clients are probably accessed remotely via dial-in modem or Internet/VPN connections. In a setting like this, the contractor's system acts as a hidden hub that spreads the malware (or any other file that is not intended for spreading, such as confidential information or licensed software). For asset owners, it is essential to make sure and verify that the endpoints of remote access at the contractor's point of presence (whether an office LAN or a portable notebook dialing in from a hotel room) cannot relay to third-party systems. In essence, hidden hubs contradict all efforts to establish a defense-in-depth architecture.

The best way to delete hidden hubs is by policy, making sure that assumed endpoints are also real endpoints.

Robustification Procedure

Step 1. *Document what you have.* For the system under consideration, document existing systems that can act as potential access points. The most important systems to consider are engineering notebooks and systems used for remote maintenance either by contractors or by staff. Document whether these are real endpoints or hidden hubs. Cooperation of contractors is essential here.

Step 2. *Document what you need.* For the system under consideration, document the potential access points that really must be endpoints. Usually, this includes all potential access points.

Step 3. *Identify and close the gaps.* Remove as many hidden hubs as practical. In many cases, this requires cooperation from contractors and vendors.

Step 4. *Document changes.* Incorporate the necessary policy changes into the document management system in place.

Step 5. *Pursue consistency and sustainability.* Communicate the policy changes to all people who are affected by them, including third parties such as contractors and vendors if applicable. Audit policy compliance regularly, including on-site audits at contractors and vendors with remote access capability.

6.6   Restricting User Access and User Interaction

Human users present one of the biggest challenges for system reliability, because the bandwidth of human behavior when interacting with cyber systems is extreme—from beneficial troubleshooting to intentional malicious attacks. Humans may destroy a system physically, install new software, change configurations, flip switches, all in a manner that may or may not be compliant with policy. The worst case here is *unrestricted user access*: Anybody can do anything. With few exceptions, such as in pharmaceuticals, user access control is often not monitored and enforced.

Fragility observed: User access and user interaction are unrestricted; the system under consideration or its subsystems are accessible by anonymous users. The system under consideration is also considered fragile if it is unknown whether it is accessible by anonymous users.

Robustification strategy: Human users present one of the biggest sources of variation for cyber systems. If user interaction is restricted to what is necessary in terms of authorization, the range of variation is reduced, and so is the chance for cybertrips.

Robustification principle: Blocking invalid input (from human actors).

Robustness target: The system under consideration is accessible only by authorized users for interactions limited by the extent of the authorization. All users for which system access is required are subject to written policy or SOPs. Access and interaction are restricted by technical means (such as locked cabinets, authentication procedures) to the extent reasonable. Policy and technical restrictions are auditable and are audited regularly. Policy violations are recorded and sanctioned.

Restricting user access does not stop with preventing unauthorized system access. It would be outright naïve to assume that authorized users with the best intent will intuitively always act in the right way without having been told what the right way is.

A contractor tries unsuccessfully to log on to a computer system on the plant floor. In an attempt to troubleshoot what appears to be a "frozen" system, the contractor reboots the system. In effect, several background processes that run on this system are stopped, which causes a production halt. Investigation determines that the contractor shouldn't have used that particular system anyway, not to mention rebooting it. There was, however, no policy addressing this circumstance. Thus, the contractor's behavior did not violate policy.

Many control system applications, such as commercial and custom-built SCADA software, are installed and configured to run with administrative credentials, simply because either the vendor or the user did not figure out how to configure such applications with restricted authorization. However, any software application or service that is executed with administrative rights must be considered malware-friendly. It is an invitation for malware to hook into such application or service in order to run with administrative rights. Such configuration also opens the opportunity to accidentally execute, delete, rename program files, change configuration settings, etc.

Policies to restrict user access and interaction should address the following questions:

- *Who?* The addressee of the policy. This may be an individual user, a user group, or a role. Rules and restrictions should be defined for *all* people with any kind of access to the system under consideration— including janitors and contractors.

- *What?* Policies assign and authorize specific tasks and explicitly prohibit any other interaction. Only interactions that are *required* for the system's functions should be permitted, which are specified in detail in the policy.

- *How?* The exact access path and method or procedure to be followed, defined physically and logically. Rules and restrictions define what access methods are authorized and what are not (physical, network, console, local media). For example, an operator may use keyboard and mouse only, while a maintenance engineer may also use transportable media. Physical access may be restricted by placing systems in locked cabinets. Network access may be limited to specific client systems by firewall rules or access control lists. Logical application/function access may be restricted to specific users or user groups by authentication/authorization schematics.

- *When?* The access context (system state), e.g., during system downtime versus at runtime.

Access policies must be auditable, and should be audited regularly—for example, every two years.

Rules and restrictions may be administrative only, or administrative with corresponding technical enforcement. Technical enforcement alone is not sufficient, because it cannot be verified; there must always be some policy document that allows assessment and verification of whether technical enforcements are appropriate and perform as specified.

Note: The term *policy* is preferred here over SOPs, because the main focus of policies is on defining legitimate usage of cyber systems. The restrictions in question may, however, also be part of an SOP. While the emphasis of this robustification strategy is on authorization, it is generally recommended to specify the *when* and *how* activity parts in a standard operation procedure as detailed below.

Robustification Procedure

Step 1. *Document what you have.* For the system under consideration, document existing system access opportunities, user intervention patterns, and use cases, ideally grouped by roles.

Step 2. *Document what you need.* For the system under consideration, document the role-based user intervention patterns that are actually required.

Step 3. *Identify and close the gaps.* Install and enforce policies to restrict user access to what is required.

Step 4. *Document changes.* Document the new policy in the appropriate document management system.

Step 5. *Pursue consistency and sustainability.* Communicate and audit the new policy.

6.7   Reducing Variation in Procedure (Standard Operating Procedures)

Many times in engineering, there is more than one way to solve a problem, and alternative approaches may even be of identical value and similar cost. If the responsibility for selecting appropriate procedures to perform a specific function is left to local staff, it can be predicted that procedures will be performed with substantial variability. This variability may lead to higher training cost, higher audit cost (if audit is even possible), and to foreseeable errors when relocating staff members. Therefore, it is a good idea to establish intraorganizational standards, or SOPs, for recurring cyber tasks, especially in areas where official standards or best practices by independent industry organizations are not available. It is easier to understand and memorize one plan of action than two, or twelve. It is much easier to verify compliance for one SOP than for two, or twelve. The more solutions there are, the greater is the probability that sooner or later someone may no longer be able to figure out how something is done, especially when responsibility changes. SOPs make sure that everybody is moving in the same direction, and eliminates time wasted in reinventing the wheel.

Fragility observed: No standards exist for typical common repetitive tasks such as remote access and backup. Such typical operations are performed according to personal preference, or not at all. The system under consideration is also considered fragile if it is not documented how common repetitive tasks are performed.

Robustification strategy: Solving similar tasks with different approaches is unnecessary variation that is bound to produce problems. Identical or at least similar procedures are much easier to verify.

Robustification principle: The consistency principle.

Robustness target: To the extent possible (i.e., without limiting required functionality under given circumstances), the organization uses documented, standardized, and auditable procedures (SOPs) to solve identical or similar repetitive tasks such as backup, remote access, or IP address allocation. The standards/documents enable other staff members or contractors to perform the procedure in an identical way. Standards and procedures are audited, and violations are sanctioned.

SOPs are very similar to policies, and sometimes there is a significant overlap between the two instruments. The major difference is that for SOPs, the emphasis is on the *when* and *how* parts of procedures, whereas policies focus on the *who* and *what* parts (corresponding to authentication and authorization).

Where no SOP exist, it can be assumed that identical tasks are performed differently by different people, or even differently by the same person on different occasions. An SOP *may* explain purpose, but it *must* be explicit on procedure. (Note: The term *standard operating procedure*, or SOP, is preferred over the term *policy*, because experience has shown that IT policies often do not address the specifics and needs of the production environment, which has led to a situation where many control engineers regard IT policies as irrelevant.)

Procedures that are prone to variation in definition and execution are often found to include *non-application-specific tasks* such as those highlighted below. Where the definition of such procedures is the responsibility of local staff or third parties, variation must be expected. If for any such recurring task there is no SOP, it cannot be expected that staff will invent identical or even similar procedures just by intuition. It is recommended that such definitions be accessible from a central repository and be subject to document management.

The procedures required to troubleshoot, repair, adapt, extend, and maintain the system should be standardized and documented to a level that they can be executed identically by a different (knowledgeable and trained) person. An organization that uses SOPs has a much higher chance of successful task completion by any engineer, not just by those who are intimately familiar with what may be idiosyncratic procedures, or who have above-average knowledge and skill. Similar to policies, SOP execution must be auditable, so that it can be determined by non-involved third parties whether execution of a specific task is in accordance with SOPs.

Some areas to focus on include the following.

- **Remote access:** For many asset owners, the specifics of remote connectivity remain the vendor's or contractor's responsibility. In such organizations, different types of remote access procedures may be found, including classic dial-in procedures by modem, as well as Internet-based VPN procedures. The details of authorized procedures are sometimes specified by policy, or they may be completely at the discretion of third parties.

- **File backup:** Backup procedures are sometimes left to local staff responsible for the system under consideration. If such a policy is used, it can be expected that backup procedures and products will vary from asset to asset, potentially resulting in situations where other staff members may be completely unfamiliar with the procedures used for similar assets. In addition, it may be debated whether a uniform or near-identical task such as backup should be performed in various ways.

- **Patch management:** Few topics show so much variation in procedure as the application of software and firmware patches. While many organizations try to patch as quickly as possible, others have given up all attempts and deliberately decided to do nothing (realizing that patches change the execution environment in a way that some fragile applications may not tolerate). The worst approach puts the decision on patch procedures in the hands of local engineers, thereby providing for variability within the organization.

A company in the automotive industry has a complex patch policy involving a structured multilayered process. When installing a specific software application on two system groups which are in essence nearly identical, it is experienced that the application runs flawlessly on one system group but not on the other. During troubleshooting it is discovered that both the two groups run different operating system patch levels, which was neither necessary nor intended.

- **System monitoring:** In the absence of corporate standards, maintenance engineers may invent creative solutions for system monitoring.

One example found by the author was a maintenance engineer who monitored logs on a backup server in order to determine whether the backup clients were operational.

Besides such idiosyncratic procedures, a variety of technical approaches exist, stretching from SNMP clients to Nagios.

- **Address and namespace management:** If the schematics of IP address allocation, hostname definition, PROFINET device names, etc., are left to the imagination of a local administrator, it can be predicted that different administrators will arrive at different solutions, thereby making maintenance more difficult than it has to be, and reducing replaceability.
- **Troubleshooting network connections:** Many maintenance engineers are left alone with their creativity to troubleshoot network connections. Those who did not enjoy a formal education in network protocols and administration may rely on trial and error to figure out what's wrong, and how to fix it. This process is time-consuming and will lead to non-standard "fixes" that may well become local "de-facto standards."
- **Handling emergencies:** Several cyber emergency scenarios can be anticipated by an organization, such as aggressive malware breakout, sabotage, sabotage attempt, and breakdown of critical cyber systems. If no plans exist for how to deal with such emergencies, it can be expected that the course of action will be taken ad hoc by local staff, acting under substantial pressure. It cannot be expected, however, that different staff

members (at different locations) will use the same measures to deal with the situation.

Robustification Procedure

Step 1. *Document what you have.* For the system under consideration, check the existing standard operating procedures. Document procedures that are executed independently by multiple people, or are executed repetitively, or both. A good starting point is procedures that are application-independent, like those mentioned above. Document any differences in procedure for identical purposes. Validate and document whether existing SOPs are executable and auditable by typical staff.

Step 2. *Document what you need.* For the system under consideration, document how many different procedure variants are required for any repetitive and/or universal task, or if any variability is mandated by requirements.

Step 3. *Identify and close the gaps.* Define as few SOPs as possible, and make sure they are practical.

Step 4. *Document changes.* Document the revised or new SOP in an appropriate document management system.

Step 5. *Pursue consistency and sustainability.* Make sure that the revised or new SOP is communicated, understood, and followed by all relevant actors, including new staff members and contractors.

6.8   Reducing Network Exposure

Unlike general-purpose office networks, the value of a process control network does not increase with the number of connected systems. Metcalfe's law states that the value of a network increases exponentially in relation to the number of connected stations. However, Metcalfe's law does not apply to process control networks. The law is very reasonable for general-purpose networks where there is an assumed intrinsic benefit for any station to be able to communicate with any other station, including anonymous systems. In process control networks, though, the potential for disturbance increases with the number of connected systems, while the value of the network remains more or less constant. Viewed in terms of cyber fragility and robustness, the idea of establishing "open" process control networks, which would eventually even be connected to the Internet, was one of the most bizarre design flaws of the 1990s.

Fragility observed: The system under consideration is network accessible by anonymous agents in an open network and can generate network traffic to arbitrary systems. The system under consideration is also considered fragile if network accessibility is undocumented.

Robustification strategy: The more systems there are that can communicate within a network, the greater is the potential for undesired and potentially hazardous network traffic to hit a specific IACS component. Limiting network exposure reduces this potential.

Robustification principle: Blocking invalid input (from technical systems).

Robustness target: The system under consideration can only be reached by required applications or services on required systems, where both systems and applications/services are verified by application-level authentication (if appropriate). The system under consideration can only reach other applications or services via a network to which connectivity is required.

Network exposure of a system to anonymous agents may result in the inability to control cyber operating parameters, because unknown agents may present a system with unpredictable input, ranging from malformed network noise to well-formed but illegitimate commands. Reducing network exposure thus means reducing the variability of input via the network, including cyber noise. Examples include:

- A broadcast storm that is initiated by a defective network interface (such as in the Browns Ferry incident)
- A legitimate application in the network that accidentally accesses the system under consideration because of misaddressing
- Malware in the network that affects the system under consideration by a DoS attack, worm propagation, or something similar

A networked system must be reachable by its specified counterparts in order to fulfill its purpose via specified transactions and transmissions.

Reachability by any other system with which interaction is not required increases the chance for traffic that results in undesired consequences. Nonrequired traffic has no place in a process control network, and it should be prevented to the extent possible.

The benefit of reducing network exposure cannot be overstated. In essence, it is twofold: First, reduced network exposure reduces the number of potential sources of problems. Second, it reduces the number of affected systems, and therefore the potential for damage.

> *Reducing network exposure of controllers is a key element in addressing the threat of post-Stuxnet malware. Such malware will not only target individual controllers, as in the case of Stuxnet itself, but will try to infect every controller that is reachable via the network. The amount of potential damage is therefore proportional to network reachability.*

Network exposure can be reduced stepwise in varying degrees, as outlined below.

- **Open network:** An "open" network is characterized by virtually zero restrictions on system accessibility. Networked systems can communicate freely with each other, and are accessible from outside the network. The network is connected to other network domains such as office or other facilities, and potentially to the Internet (worst case).

- **Zoned network:** The network is divided in functional zones that may continue to function if another zone is down (e.g., because of malware infection). Only very limited access is possible into zones, while data flow within a zone is unrestricted.

  The robustness of a zoned network can be increased by making zones as small as possible. This is usually achieved in a process that may extend over several years. Many asset owners start with a zoning strategy by separating the process network from the business network. The next level is then to divide the process network even further, into multiple zones.

- **System-level point-to-point restriction:** Network data flow is limited to connections which are required to fulfill the specified functions. Systems that do not need to exchange data with the system under consideration cannot reach it. This type of restriction is executed on a systems level, e.g., through IP addressing.

- **Application-level point-to-point restriction:** The system under consideration can only be reached by systems, applications, and services which are required to talk to the SUC per specification. This type of restriction is executed on an application level, e.g., through TCP/UDP port numbers (best case).

Robustification Procedure

Step 1. *Document what you have.* For the system under consideration, document the existing interfaces to networked systems (= network reachability). The integrator may be a big help here.

Step 2. *Document what you need.* For the system under consideration, document the network communication paths that are actually required.

Step 3. *Identify and close the gaps.* Reduce as many nonrequired network traffic paths as possible by access control lists, zoning, or application-level firewalls.

Step 4. *Document changes.* Document the new system configuration.

Step 5. *Pursue consistency and sustainability.* Make sure that any new identical or similar system uses a "least reachability" configuration from the start.

6.9   Reducing Variation in Equipment Type, Product Version, and Configuration Options

In mid-size and large installations, usually more than one system is used for similar or identical tasks. For example, multiple PLCs are installed to control one assembly line. Where multiple assembly lines, machines, and plants are installed, one may find multiple SCADA or DCS applications. For all but the most specialized automation tasks, it is possible to source different products from different vendors, or different products from the same vendor. Such different products may well be mixed. However, different models and products vary in configuration interfaces, user interfaces, engineering tools, etc., and impose higher cost on keeping spare parts, testing, and education.

Fragility observed: No standards limit the options for equipment sourcing and configuration.

Robustification strategy: Using different equipment or configurations for similar purposes creates unnecessary variation. It may also lead to version conflicts.

Robustification principle: The consistency principle.

Robustness target: To the extent possible and reasonable, without limiting required functionality under given circumstances, the organization procures the least possible number of different equipment and product versions from the least possible number of vendors. There are formal and detailed specifications (standards) on how to configure systems, including software and middleware, thereby limiting configuration options to the number required to fulfill given requirements.

Many larger organizations use equipment regulations for procurement in which approved vendors and products (along with model identification) are listed. Limiting the number of equipment vendors for a specific product category to one is usually considered counterproductive for pricing and availability reasons—lack of competition might raise prices—and if that one source should experience delivery problems or ultimately go out of business, the asset owner might have serious problems. For these reasons, most larger asset owners favor a "second source" strategy, which is essentially a surplus strategy as discussed in the next chapter.

Equipment regulations should extend to configuration. Modern IACS have numerous configuration options for flexibility. If such configuration options are not limited by policy, it can be expected that identical systems are operated with different configurations. This is another example of installing cyber tripwires.

Serial RS-232/422 and current loop links used to be prone to configuration diversity. If a maintenance engineer has an option to select different transmission speeds, framing types, number of stop bits, and/or flow control procedures, then it can be expected that different parameters will be selected for similar systems. It is then only a question of time until noncompatible settings are configured just by accident or because some other maintenance engineer "always uses that setting." If configuration settings are fixed per equipment regulation, this source of variability—and errors—is eliminated.

Note: In a procedural view, this strategy can also be seen as a candidate for standard operating procedures, which do not apply only to operations but also to planning, procurement, and configuration.

Robustification Procedure

Step 1. *Document what you have.* For the system under consideration, document how many different variants of equipment type exist for similar or identical purposes.

Step 2. *Document what you need.* For the system under consideration, document how many different variants of equipment type are required.

Step 3. *Identify and close the gaps.* Make sure that at end-of-lifetime, systems and products that did not make the cut are replaced by the new standard.

Step 4. *Document changes.* Document the new system configuration.

Step 5. *Pursue consistency and sustainability.* Incorporate the new standard into your procurement specification.

Chapter 7

Enforcing and Reinforcing Structure

As long as ideal conditions are expected all the time, throughout a system's lifecycle, it may be reasonable to go for lean design. However, preparing for unfavorable conditions (contingencies) requires excess material, energy, manpower, coding, etc. In a best-case scenario, such excess is never needed—it just sits idle and produces nothing but cost. Where specific functionality is mission-critical, it is a good idea not to rely on best-case assumptions to materialize all the time, especially where external factors exist that cannot be controlled or even be predicted accurately. *Surplus strategies* account for the potential for unfavorable conditions, even if they are uncertain and hard to predict. It may be relatively pointless to search for probable causes in such situations.

Just like reduction strategies, surplus strategies center on functionality and resources that are not needed for normal operation under normal conditions. Surplus strategies are in some way the opposite of reduction strategies, as they are not about cutting back, but about adding to what is already there, and to what could be sufficient in a perfect world. However, here it's about the capability to continue operation in the face of contingencies. Surplus strategies don't deliver more functionality and don't increase performance, but they do deliver core functionality under more conditions. They are "fat" strategies—the opposite of "lean" strategies.

Reduction strategies are applied where there is the *potential* for optimizing reliability and maintainability; surplus strategies are applied where there is the *need*. As another difference between surplus strategies and reduction strategies, there is no absolute upper limit for surplus strategies. Reduction strategies have to stop when the bare bones of required functionality are reached. Beyond that point, reduction is counterproductive. For surplus strategies, more is always better. For example, hot-standby redundancy is better than having an inventory of spare parts for every system, which is better than having only one spare per model. Triple redundancy is better than double redundancy; for resilience, it is better to use a million test cases for fuzzing than ten thousand, and so forth.

Nevertheless, reduction strategies and surplus strategies have in common that the goal is to close any gaps between observed and required system configuration. In the case of reduction strategies, this is achieved by cutting away nonrequired functionality, whereas in the case of surplus strategies, it is achieved by adding resources and *application-neutral functionality* for reliability in contingency situations. Since surplus functionality and resources are not used in normal situations, the availability and accuracy of these functions and resources should be monitored and verified regularly. This is well known from safety: The reliability of a function that is executed only once every thousand hours is difficult to assess. Especially, procedural surplus (such as backup/restore) should be checked periodically.

Surplus strategies can basically be grouped into three categories with respect to the problem area that they address:

1. *System-level faults and stress conditions.* This group of strategies aims at binary and analog contingencies.

2. *Detecting and handling erroneous runtime data, configuration changes, and program code.* This group of strategies aims at the digital contingency layer.

3. *Preventing undesired effects from undetermined problem sources.* The last group of strategies is a catchall which acknowledges that not all contingencies may be prepared for properly. It's a "no matter why" approach.

The following sections illustrate several best-practice surplus strategies.

7.1 Resilient Code and Architecture

The term *resilience* in the context of networked IACS usually refers to the ability to tolerate malformed or otherwise unexpected data. Such data may be online data that hits the system's network interface—both malformed and well formed (but unexpected by the developer), or corrupt configuration files, which may result, for example, from accidental network misaddressing.

Fragility observed: Malformed data and/or data that is well formed but unexpected for the SUC (e.g., empty UDP packets, ICMP, broadcasts) may negatively affect system performance and behavior. The system under consideration is also considered fragile if its resilience is unknown.

Robustification strategy: Robustness is increased by checking the syntactic validity of data before processing, by adding code for handling exceptions, and by a system architecture that tolerates unexpected (though legitimate) network traffic.

Robustification principle: Limit transfer function range (application level).

Robustness target: Network and configuration resilience are tested and documented. Based on test results, system performance is not affected by corrupt or unexpected, out-of-protocol data that hit networked systems and subsystems.

Resilience is about the syntactical aspects of the "garbage in, garbage out" problem. For IACS, it is important to make sure that "garbage in" will not result in "garbage out." Some systems are even stressed by completely well-formed data (such as network scans) that the system developer simply did not consider. This leads to the problem that standard-conformant data, such as empty packets or broadcasts, may fail a system simply because it isn't handled properly in the driver's implementation. Therefore, it doesn't help to look at Internet RFCs, for example, to determine if specific network traffic could cause trouble with certain devices or not—it's completely up to the implementation, thus to product and version. Since "good" data and "bad" data are not identifiable with respect to RFCs or similar standards, it is impossible to determine what "bad" data would be without referring to a specific system and version. It may be questioned, however, whether any contemporary product which claims to be Ethernet and TCP/IP compatible must be considered defective if it is unable to tolerate network scans, broadcasts, etc.

What makes network resilience difficult is the fact that protocol integrity stretches through multiple layers which are usually implemented by different people in different organizations—for example, Ethernet layer (NIC imple-menter), TCP/IP transport layer (implementer of IP stack), and application layer (product or application vendor).

Fuzzing

Several commercial and noncommercial test frameworks are available to test network resilience. The best-known approach to doing this is *fuzzing*. Fuzzers deliberately alter network packet structure, information in proto-col header fields, etc., to determine whether the tested system is able to tolerate such alterations. For example, it is well known that many auto-mation peripherals, even contemporary models, are not capable of surviv-ing simple network scans, which are performed by software tools that are considered standard equipment for network administrators and that do not necessarily emit completely malformed packets. This problem has led to a situation where most asset owners prohibit the use of network scanners in process networks, thereby taking away a very valuable tool from their network administrators.

Resilient Code

The assumption that any data traffic from the network that hits a system is always and only what the target device expects at the given moment is highly unrealistic, especially in "open" process control networks, where the SUC may be hit with data from stations that have no business communicating with the SUC anyway. A nonresilient software or firmware program may work fine as long as the data consumed is completely well formed and as expected. However, the developer has only taken care of the ideal case, where data is 100% intact, timely, in sequence, and valid for the given context; there is no exception handling. Thus, if these assumption do not hold, system behavior is usually unpredictable.

Resilient code checks the validity of data before processing. While this may seem straightforward and almost natural, it is not easy to implement. Overhead for handling exceptions can be significant, and exception handling does not deliver tangible functionality to users. Perhaps this is reason enough why often it's simply not done. In many cases, the best course of action for an IACS is to ignore a (network-induced) exception. What is required in any case is that the execution of the control logic is not affected.

Resilient Architecture

Resilient architecture refers to a system architecture that is not sensitive to well-formed and legitimate, but irrelevant—and therefore unexpected—data. Examples are ICMP packets, broadcast packets, or TCP SYN packets, packets with a data length of zero. All these are typical data that network scanners may transmit and that are not considered malicious or dangerous in contemporary networks. IACS components may have problems when hit by such data, just for performance reasons (analog contingency layer). This is especially the case for product architectures that do the processing of network traffic on the same CPU that executes the application.

Combinatorial Leverage

One strategy to enhance resilience is authentication. If it can be verified that network commands and configuration files are authentic and legitimate, the extent of syntax and semantics checking before processing the data may be reduced.

Robustification Procedure

Step 1. *Document what you have.* For the system under consideration, document the existing resilience. To do this, define and use appropriate test tools. The vendor may help.

Step 2. *Document what you need.* For the system under consideration, document the type of resilience that is actually required. This may, for example, include requirements for undisturbed I/O behavior while the system's network interface is stressed by broadcast storms and fuzzers.

Step 3. *Identify and close the gaps.* If possible, increase the resilience of the system under consideration. In many cases, this can only be done by the vendor. If not possible, choose an alternative product with adequate resilience. If that is also not possible, it may be necessary to mandate a highly restricted network environment (see Section 6.8).

Step 4. *Document changes.* Document the new system configuration.

Step 5. *Pursue consistency and sustainability.* Make sure that any new identical or similar system uses the resilient configuration or product from the start.

7.2   Code Execution and Configuration Tamper Control/Monitoring

Code and configuration control is complementary to system hardening. Even though the goal of code and configuration control is to restrict which applications can be executed on the target system and who can make changes to configuration files, extra (surplus) logic is installed to control just that. Surplus functionality is introduced that controls code and configuration data on the target system, to make sure that only legitimate code is executed and that the configuration is not changed either accidentally or maliciously.

Fragility observed: No barrier prevents unauthorized software being installed and executed on the system under consideration. Configuration changes are not checked for authorization. The system under consideration is also considered fragile if it is not documented in which way software is restricted from installation and execution.

Robustification strategy: Limitations on code and data changes on the system under configuration prevent both malicious and accidental changes from being processed.

Robustification principle: Limit transfer function range (system level).

Robustness target: No unauthorized or unvalidated software programs, configuration files, etc., can be installed and processed on the system under consideration.

Commercial product implementations that can be used to employ this strategy come in different alternatives as discussed below.

Host-Based Intrusion Detection Systems

Host-based intrusion detection systems (HIDS) have been around for many years. Even though the names are similar, HIDS have little to do with network intrusion detection systems. The basic function of a HIDS is to check configuration integrity. A HIDS basically monitors the file system(s) of a computer system for changes. Any detected changes are reported to an administrator, who may then determine whether the changes are authorized. Basically, HIDS aim at configuration tamper monitoring.

In 2008, a German company in the dairy industry was the victim of a sabotage attack with the goal of extortion. The attackers threatened to spoil the victim's products by lowering the temperature of the pasteurization process, and they made that threat credible by a demonstration. They demanded a multimillion dollar ransom. The attack could be countered because a HIDS was in place. Examination of HIDS logs enabled the victim, with the help of professional crime fighters, to identify the attacking application.

Configuration tamper monitoring (either standalone or as part of HIDS) would also have detected Stuxnet because of the files that Stuxnet changed, copied, and renamed.

PLC Version Control

PLC version control systems and integrity monitors can be thought of as a complementary to HIDS for controllers. In a way, monitoring the integrity of a controller is easier than monitoring the integrity of a computer system, because most controllers don't have a file system.

PLC version control systems have been around for several years. Usually they are used in a workgroup environment, where multiple developers who work on a specific PLC program check their code changes in a manner that has been known in software development for decades. In addition, the version control system automatically downloads the programs that are running on the monitored PLCs periodically (usually once per day) and compares the actual program code with what the version control system thinks should be running on the PLC, according to its change management database. Any mismatches are reported and can be analyzed for changes against the configuration that should be running.

Controller Integrity Monitoring

A stripped-down alternative to a PLC version control system is a PLC integrity monitoring system. It only detects configuration changes, without necessarily telling what those changes are. The benefit compared to a full-blown PLC version control system is that a PLC integrity monitor doesn't download the complete program code and data from the PLC, which is time-consuming and may even reduce PLC processing power during the download. While it is not feasible to scan PLCs with version control systems every minute or so, this can be done with an integrity monitor. If an integrity monitor detects a potentially unscheduled and unauthorized configuration change, maintenance engineers can explore the details of the change using existing tools, such as the vendor's development environment or an existing version control system.

> *Both PLC version control systems and PLC integrity monitoring would have detected the rogue ladder logic injected on controllers by Stuxnet easily, given that they used independent software drivers to access the PLC rather than relying on the compromised vendor's driver DLL.*

Antivirus Solutions

Modern antivirus solutions try to prevent the installation and execution of malware by pattern matching and by behavioral analysis. The latter is a bit unreliable. For pattern matching, an antivirus solution matches signatures for any executable file that is introduced to a computer system against a list of signatures for known malware—a blacklist. Whichever program is identified in the blacklist is prevented from being installed and executed. In addition, an alert is issued to the user.

A problem with antivirus products for production environments is that they require antivirus signature updates multiple times per day, and they may change the execution environment significantly, triggering analog contingency situations where, for example, real-time behavior is compromised. It has to be acknowledged that because of such problems, many asset owners have chosen to run their computer systems with no antivirus software, especially after having encountered performance and reliability problems of the application that the antivirus solution was intended to protect. After uninstalling antivirus software, more than one maintenance engineer has been pleasantly surprised by the performance boost on the system.

Another problem is the potential for false-positive alarms.

> *In April 2010, signature update 5958 of antivirus vendor McAfee provoked systems running Windows XP to constantly reboot, because a Windows system file was false-positively identified as malicious and put into quarantine. In production environments, such behavior will most likely result in downtime.*

Whitelisting Solutions

Similar to antivirus, whitelisting technology aims at preventing the execution of unauthorized software, but it uses a whitelist rather than a blacklist. Just like conventional antivirus software, signatures are computed for executable programs. These signatures are then compared to a list of legitimate software applications and drivers. If no match is found, the software in question is blocked from execution. Whitelisting is thus much more strict on execution control: It prevents not only malware from being executed, but also any other kind of unauthorized software, such as games, media players, etc.

Whitelisting solutions are most noteworthy here because of the following characteristics that make them appealing to process control environments.

- In addition to preventing the installation of known malware (which is the main purpose of classic antivirus solutions), they also prevent installation of unknown malware and of nonmalicious but unauthorized applications (such as media players and other recreational software that users tend to install on systems even in production environments).
- The whitelisting approach also has a lot of appeal for control systems, because these systems tend to be static over many years, with the ideal system state being identical to the state of commissioning. Whitelisting solutions provide a way to "freeze" a system in just such a configuration.

It is well known that Stuxnet exploited four zero-day vulnerabilities that allowed it to spread among systems with antivirus solutions installed and current AV signatures. A whitelisting solution would most likely have prevented Stuxnet from executing and spreading.

In environments where configuration changes and updates occur frequently, such as in the average office IT environment, whitelisting solutions lack utility.

Intrusion Prevention Systems

Intrusion prevention systems (IPS) blend the approaches mentioned above into a more complex solution to block unauthorized software from being executed and files from being changed without authorization. So far, IPS are rarely seen on control systems, mostly because they are fairly difficult to configure, and because existing IPS products are designed for office IT environments.

Robustification Procedure

Step 1. *Document what you have.* For the system under consideration, document the existing methods of code execution and configuration tamper control. Note that since Stuxnet, controllers must be included.

Step 2. *Document what you need.* For the system under consideration, document the type of code execution and configuration tamper control required.

Step 3. *Identify and close the gaps.* Test and install additional methods of code execution and configuration tamper control. Testing may be omitted if the application vendor has certified the selected solution(s).

Step 4. *Document changes.* Document the new system configuration.

Step 5. *Pursue consistency and sustainability.* Make sure that any identical or similar system uses the selected method of code and configuration tamper control.

7.3   Encoding and Verifying Meta Information for End-to-End Validity Checking

Resilience (as detailed earlier) does nothing with respect to well-formed, legitimate data that may be out of context, accidentally sent to the wrong system, accidentally assuming a wrong configuration, or that has malicious intent. Such situations may be prevented easily by encoding *meta information*. Meta information may include digital signatures, command sequence numbers, data source and target identifiers, or application-level confirmation messages.

Fragility observed: Due to the layered architecture of popular network protocols, meta information that would potentially allow the receiving system or application to check for the validity of commands may be scattered across different layers of the protocol stack. This may lead to situations where erroneous messages cannot be detected by the target application and, if processed, will likely result in a cybertrip.

Robustification strategy: Robustness is increased by checking the content validity of firmware, code, commands, parameters, etc., before processing. This can be achieved by encoding meta information.

Robustification principle: Limit transfer function range.

Robustness target: Erroneous (syntactically correct, but improper) files and messages can be detected by checking meta information and will not be processed.

Causes for cybertrips are sometimes surprisingly trivial, especially those associated with accidental user interaction. For example, many maintenance engineers have reconfigured or reprogrammed the wrong system, which may happen quickly if no physical proximity is required, thanks to networking. The target system has no way to check the validity of commands if everything is well formed from a syntactic point of view. Prime candidates for such meta information are listed below.

- **Firmware for automation peripherals:** Contemporary automation peripherals allow for loading firmware via the network interface. If a corrupt firmware image is loaded on a peripheral, this may result in the device becoming nonfunctional, requiring it to be sent to the factory for repair.

  The U.S. Department of Homeland Security addressed this issue in 2007 by "semi-publishing" information (categorized for official use only) on a vulnerability which was dubbed "Boreas." Boreas is about rogue firmware that is loaded to automation peripherals via the network in order to make them nonfunctional. A victim would likely experience very high damage in this case, as most installations have only limited spares per model available on site.

- **Program code:** For program code and drivers, it has become customary in the Microsoft Windows environment that such code is digitally signed. At the controller level, this is not the case. Most controllers accept any program file that is syntactically correct, without any checks for authenticity.

  It is well known that Stuxnet used stolen digital certificates for signing Windows program code.

  At the PLC level, stealing certificates was not necessary for the developers of Stuxnet because the automation products that were used to carry out the attack didn't support signed code. If they had, the attack would have been more difficult or even impossible to execute. With respect to the threat of post-Stuxnet malware, it must be assumed that stolen digital certificates for computer programs will remain the exception, while rogue ladder logic will be seen more frequently. Provisions for digitally signing controller code will help to counter this threat.

- Online commands and parameters: Controllers rarely work fully auton-omous and standalone. Often they are monitored and supervised by human operators using operator panels or SCADA HMI workstations, where process conditions are changed and process parameters such as setpoints are manipulated.

Technically, setpoints for a specific machine or reactor are frequently changed by writing directly to PLC memory. If the engineer uses obsolete configuration information, data will be written at the wrong memory address, while the PLC will most likely acknowledge a successful write operation. Systems which provide some form of symbolic command language would be able to catch this error, because mapping from symbols to memory locations would be performed by the target system.

Technically, the XML standard has become an accepted and flexible way to code meta information. This standard is beginning to be used for configuration files. There are also protocols for transmitting live process data encoded in XML, for example, the FactoryXML command language and protocol invented by the author.

Robustification Procedure

Step 1. *Document what you have.* For the system under consider-ation, document the existing methods for checking code and con-figuration authenticity by meta information. The vendor or integrator may help.

Step 2. *Document what you need.* For the system under consideration, document the required methods for checking code and configuration authenticity by meta information.

Step 3. *Identify and close the gaps.* If possible, incorporate better methods for checking code and configuration authenticity by meta information, probably by switching to another product or another vendor.

Step 4. *Document changes.* Document the new system configuration.

Step 5. *Pursue consistency and sustainability.* Make sure that any new identical or similar system uses the selected method for end-to-end validity checking of code and commands.

7.4   Context-Based Restrictions on Control Authority (Inherent Safety)

Context-based restrictions on control authority are similar to role-based authorization concepts. The major difference is that limitations of authority are based not only on actor identity (as determined by authentication and association with a specific role) but also extend to system state.

Fragility observed: Cyber commands may execute the full function set at any time, even when function execution would make no sense in the given state or would be outright unsafe. The system under consideration is also considered fragile if it is undocumented whether the full function set can be executed regardless of system state.

Robustification strategy: Preventing operating modes that can *only* result in undesired behavior reduces the probability of undesired input resulting in undesired consequences, no matter who did it (i.e., without taking authentication and authorization into account).

Robustification principle: Limiting transfer function range.

Robustness target: The system under consideration technically limits control authority to functions that are safe and legitimate for the given operating mode or system state. Remote access cannot result in process manipulations that local operators are not aware of, or that would put the system under consideration or the governed process in an unsafe state.

In some industrial automation and control applications, the traditional IT concept of authentication and authorization lacks granularity because it is context-free. Usually, a person or software process with administrator credentials, such as a maintenance engineer or any IT process running with "admin" rights, can do anything *at any time*—even if a specific cyber operation may have catastrophic consequences when commanded at the "wrong" time. In situations like these, it is beneficial to limit control authority based on context. This strategy is a good example of how reduction strategies and surplus strategies overlap. While the goal of the strategy is reduction, it is listed as a surplus strategy because for most contemporary products, this type of functionality must be regarded as an add-on.

It takes little consideration to determine that the assumption of maintenance staff or operators always acting accurately, even under stress, is highly unrealistic. Unintentional and/or incorrect actions by authorized and trained people are typical for any complex production environment. An authorized person may issue legitimate commands (either intentionally or not) that do not make sense for a given state of the system and can only result in damage. This is especially important for remote maintenance network connections, where it is easy to lose situational awareness of the particular state the target system is in.

While this may sound like a case for independent external safety systems, the concept of inherent safety is about preventing a dangerous command from being executed in the first place. By robust design of the automation system, much can be done to prevent a safety system from activating. Inherent safety does not reflect the specific physics or chemistry of the governed process, but the range of executable functionality in a given state. An example is limiting the execution of certain "debug" functions in fully automated run mode, because such functions are usually associated with deep manipulations that are rarely safe when executed on a "hot" system.

In aircraft equipped with fly-by-wire control, command execution is dependent on the "control law" (or system state) in which the aircraft is operating. There are different "control laws" for taxiing, takeoff, departure, cruising, and landing. Control laws prevent commands being executed that would put the aircraft in an unsafe state. For example, it is impossible to roll an Airbus, because control input in flight cannot result in further aileron deflection beyond a safe angle of bank.

Inherent safety restrictions are especially beneficial for network and remote access, where the operating context of the target system may be easily misinterpreted. For remote access to field-level controllers, the easiest way to implement inherent safety is an electromechanical switch on the system under consideration, which selects system states (e.g., run modes) and thus control laws. It then requires physical proximity to select state and thereby limits control authority to what is considered safe. Unfortunately, the general trend has been to do without such switches (in controllers), mainly for quite insignificant cost savings (in the one-digit dollar range).

The majority of state-of-the-art PLCs and controllers allow for unrestricted unauthenticated memory access via the network at any time. This includes accidental or malicious write access to memory areas that will inevitably result in severe and potentially unsafe process manipulations.

Many PLCs have electromechanical switches to set the run mode physically on the unit. Some have the additional capability to change the run mode via the network with specific commands. Therefore, a run mode that was set by local staff may be overwritten via the network. In consequence, functions may be performed that may be unsafe for the run mode that local staff had activated for good reasons.

A related problem is the ability to identify configuration settings that may have large implications to process control and process safety.

Among the most aggressive attack techniques used by Stuxnet was the disabling of automatic process image updates via a legitimate configuration setting. Operators had no indication of the configuration change that implied severe compromise of digital safety.

Robustification Procedure

Step 1. *Document what you have.* For the system under consideration, document any existing context-based restrictions of control authority. The vendor and integrator may help.

Step 2. *Document what you need.* For the system under consideration, document any required context-based restrictions of control authority.

Step 3. *Identify and close the gaps.* Restrict control authority based on context where it is required and not done already. In many cases, this can only be done by the vendor.

Step 4. *Document changes.* Document the new system configuration.

Step 5. *Pursue consistency and sustainability.* Make sure that any new identical or similar system uses the selected method of restricting control authority from the start.

7.5   Safeguards and Process Monitoring

Safeguards are sometimes called "physical/chemical exception handling." They are control systems that make sure that the results of IACS malfunctions do not cause physical damage or hurt people.

Fragility observed: Hazardous out-of-limits states that the governed process may reach can only be prevented manually (if at all) by trained staff executing the right procedures at the right time. The system under consideration is also considered fragile if it is unknown whether sufficient safeguards are in place and how they would function.

Robustification strategy: Safeguards as defined here are controls that limit the effects of out-of-bounds situations which should never occur under normal conditions. Acknowledging the uncertainty of environmental circumstances and the damage potential of certain out-of-bounds effects, safeguards may be installed to prevent such effects from happening.

Robustification principle: Block invalid output.

Robustness target: Potentially dangerous out-of-limits process states are automatically prevented, ultimately by triggering an automated controlled process shutdown.

Under best-case circumstances, safeguards are never activated, making an excellent case for the nature of surplus strategies. Safeguards are well understood, and their usage is regulated and mandatory in several configurations and applications (for example, those under monitoring by OSHA). They are mentioned here to point out that safety systems are one more way to increase the robustness of a process, and that cybertrips are one other reason why a safety system might engage.

SIS and Common Mode Failures

In a nutshell, the purpose of a digital safety system is ultimately to shut down the process in an organized manner if specific parameters exceed their thresholds, or if other hazardous events are detected. It is essential to ensure that safeguards cannot be affected by a common mode failure of the IACS—reason enough for some to argue that the respective controllers should not share the same network with IACS components.

One of the most serious aspects of Stuxnet was that it demonstrated the capability to compromise digital safety systems. Stuxnet performs a man-in-the-middle attack on a controller, providing the legitimate control code with fake input data that had been prerecorded by Stuxnet's rogue code. This attack results in the legitimate code, including all safety functions, being unable to see the reality of actual sensor values. It even works on fail-safe controllers.

Monitoring

Monitoring comes in two major flavors: Process monitoring and condition monitoring. While the first monitors process variables and their thresholds, the latter monitors asset conditions and is usually implemented as a building block of preventive maintenance.

Process monitoring by SCADA or DCS applications is a low-cost, low-profile alternative to automated safeguards. Such applications have the ability to define thresholds for process variables that will trigger alarms if exceeded. Unlike automated safeguards, this architecture relies on the presence, vigilance, and education of human operators who may take corrective action if alarms are triggered.

> *By blinding controller code, Stuxnet not only managed to lever out safety logic, but also to blind operators in the control room and any SCADA/DCS alarms.*
>
> *A major factor in the 2003 East Coast power blackout was an unnoticed failure of the alarming and monitoring software application at the utility operator, which resulted in false display of monitored values and in alarms not being displayed, thereby blinding operators from what was actually going on.*

Condition monitoring, on the other hand, monitors asset parameters (such as lubrication levels), not process variables.

Robustification Procedure

Step 1. *Document what you have.* For the system under consideration, document the existing safeguards. The integrator may help.

Step 2. *Document what you need.* For the system under consideration, document the safeguards or monitoring and alarming functions required. A guideline might be fault tree analysis.

Step 3. *Identify and close the gaps.* Implement additional safeguards or monitoring/alarming functionality. In many cases, this can only be done by the integrator.

Step 4. *Document changes.* Document the new system configuration.

Step 5. *Pursue consistency and sustainability.* Make sure that any new identical or similar system uses the same safeguards from the start.

7.6 Redundancy

Virtually every system, service, or data set that serves a nontrivial purpose requires a redundancy strategy of some kind, because zero redundancy will mean that the functionality is lost in the event of failure and cannot be resumed. Thus, the functionality of this system will no longer be available. In real life, this should apply only to nonessential systems, which have little reason to exist in an IACS environment in the first place. Systems that provide required functionality with no redundancy strategy indicate a serious fragility problem.

Fragility observed: A system, service, data set, application, or transport has no backup and cannot be timely and sufficiently replaced or restored in the event of failure. The system under consideration is also considered fragile if it is unknown how and when functionality can be restored after failure.

Robustification strategy: Provide for backup capability in the event that a system or parts thereof become unavailable for whatever reason. The backup will (try to) resume functionality identical to the original system.

Robustification principle: Adequate execution resources allocation (binary contingency layer).

Robustness target: Sufficient redundancy is provided to ensure that required MTTR is achievable at any time.

Redundancy may be applied to data processing, data transmission, and data storage resources. Essentially, it relies on the duplication of a system or parts thereof in order to continue operation in the event of failure. It is a well-known concept in engineering which applies to cyber as well. For cost optimization, redundancy may be implemented at different levels, depending on availability requirements for the functionality provided by the system in question. Redundancy may even be provided by contract—the contractor then replaces a defect system, usually including reconfiguration and system restart.

Common Mode Failures

Just as for safeguards, redundancy strategies should include analysis and specification of failure modes that are handled by the system and those that are not—i.e., common mode failures. For example, redundant cabling is of little use if all cables are using the same tray, and redundant computer systems may fail simultaneously due to broadcast storms, malware, etc.

> *A redundant DCS server was brought down by a simple OPC item browse due to resource starvation. After the primary server locked up, the secondary server took over and was also taken down by the ongoing browse operation. As a result, production in a sugar mill came to a complete halt for several hours.*
>
> *An asset owner configured a production data center with redundant server systems and performed backups regularly. However, redundant systems, backup servers, and backup tapes were all located within the same fire area. Therefore, the redundancy strategy would be worthless in case of a fire.*

Mean Time to Recover

The central metric for determining the required and achieved level of redundancy is *mean time to recover* (MTTR). MTTR is the elapsed time from system failure to complete recovery, expressed in milliseconds, seconds, minutes, or hours. In practical terms, what matters is gross MTTR. Gross MTTR is composed additively of the following factors:

1. Failure detection.

2. Problem diagnosis. If the cause of the malfunction is not determined before a backup system is administered, the backup system may experience identical problems and fail instantly (see the preceding section on common mode failures).

3. Removing the failed component. Depending on the controlled process, this may be delayed by having to stop the process, waiting for aggregates to cool down, getting to the failed component.

4. Obtaining a replacement component. Depending on the logistics, this step may occur instantly (because a backup system is already installed and configured in place), or it may be infinite in the case of obsolete components that are no longer available for purchase.

5. Configuration and testing of the replacement component. Sometimes the longest phase of recovery is configuring the replacement component—especially if configuration files are not hot-pluggable or network-installable.

6. Installation of the replacement component.

7. Restarting the affected process.

MTTR may be less than 1 second for hot-standby systems, and may be infinite for obsolete systems for which no spares are available and the vendor is no longer in business, the developer left the organization years ago, etc. Many maintenance engineers also look at the number of identical systems for redundancy planning, taking into account the risk of simultaneous failure.

Data Processing

For data processing systems, the highest level of availability is achieved by *hot-backup* standby systems that provide for uninterrupted performance even if the original system goes down. *Cold-backup* systems are in place and configured, but must be activated manually to resume operation of the original system, resulting in a window of nonavailability.

The least-cost strategy is to have spares available that must be configured for a specific purpose and then brought into place and started. For example, industrial controllers are usually not installed 100% with hot-backup redundancy, because it is assumed to be highly unlikely that all controllers will fail simultaneously. Therefore, redundancy strategies in many plants usually limit controller redundancy to a low number of units per model. While it is economical, a flaw in this strategy is that it does not provide for common-cause failures, which may be introduced easily by cyber.

> A scenario that places a very high burden on redundancy strategies is the Boreas vulnerability, i.e., maliciously altered firmware loaded to controllers that basically makes the controllers useless and prohibit reset by the user. An actual Boreas attack would require the asset owner to replace all infected controllers—after having made sure that subsequent infections are impossible.

Data Transmission

Network cabling is usually done redundantly for backbone segments but not for satellite links. In automation and control, however, essential network traffic may never pass through a backbone segment but only through satellite links, especially peer-to-peer traffic among automation peripherals.

A cost-saving strategy for networks is to use an open ring topology (with redundancy manager) rather than a redundant tree.

For active network components, the same guidelines apply as for data processing (see above).

Data Storage

For data storage, RAID systems are usually configured only for critical data, whereas other applications may get along with incremental backups. Procedural redundancy is associated with typical problems of inconsistent discipline, especially when not audited. For procedural redundancy (e.g., backup/restore), the success rate of recovery should be measured and evaluated. Backup strategies may open up room for fine-tuning, such as determining when full backups and when incremental backups are performed.

Fail-Safe Systems

Fail-safe systems with voting strategies (such as two-out-of-three, or 2oo3) are an area where redundancy concepts and strategies have been studied thoroughly. This topic is so large that it cannot be covered in detail here. It is, however, suggested to check such concepts for an in-depth understanding of redundancy.

Robustification Procedure

Step 1. *Document what you have.* For the system under consideration and for the function or asset under consideration, determine and document mean time to recover. Use an estimate if statistics are not available. Depending on system type, MTTR determination may be done separately for data processing, data storage, and data transmission.

Step 2. *Document what you need.* For the system under consideration and for the function or asset under consideration, document the required mean time to recover.

Step 3. *Identify and close the gaps.* Install additional redundancy as required.

Step 4. *Document changes.* Document the new system configuration.

Step 5. *Pursue consistency and sustainability.* Make sure that any new identical or similar system uses identical redundancy strategies from the start.

7.7   Derating (Performance Reserves)

Among the best-known robustification strategies is the allocation of reserves and performance safety margins. In normal operations and under normal circumstances, reserves will never be used—by definition, they are the excess/surplus beyond what is required for normal operation. Should conditions be different from ideal for whatever reason, reserves allow continuing operation.

Fragility observed: The system under consideration or its subsystems have insufficient or unknown resource reserves; any additional load may cause the system to trip. The system under consideration is also considered fragile if it is undocumented what kind of resource reserves exist.

Robustification strategy: Preventing to reach or exceed unreliable system limits by providing for more resources than would be needed under normal conditions, or by utilizing resources below specified limits.

Robustification principle: Adequate execution of resources allocation (analog contingency layer).

Robustness target: The system under consideration and its subsystems have enough resource reserves to perform fully under any projected extra load throughout the system's lifecycle as specified.

Allocating performance reserves beyond best-case assumptions is almost identical to *derating*—limiting performance below what would technically be possible or using components below specification. In mechanical and electrical engineering, it is customary to build in excess in order to accommodate for heavier loads than anticipated. For cyber, the idea is not to understress components (as there is little need to worry about increased wear, thermal problems, etc.), but to provide capacity for performance in contingency situations.

One should assume that providing adequate performance for IACS installations is not a big deal because such installations are very static. Since the majority of applications don't change much over their long lifecycle, neither do performance requirements. However, three factors regularly lead to typical performance-related problems: Convergence with IT applications, insufficient and outdated hardware, and lack of monitoring.

- Convergence with IT applications is easiest be observed with respect to antivirus solutions. On many plant floor systems, antivirus software has become the most demanding software process in terms of memory usage and CPU consumption. Other examples are the convergence of network applications, such as voice-over-IP and video streaming in plant networks.

- Even though hardware for data processing, transport, and storage is cheap today, many systems on real plant floors are considerably low on resources. This is partly due to the long lifetime of such systems. While it is customary for office IT systems to be upgraded every three to five years, plant floor systems may be in use for more than a decade, leading to significant differences in system quality between IT and operations. Some organizations have also established a culture that assumes that since control is more about electrics than IT, sophisticated, powerful, and expensive hardware is not needed on the plant floor, resulting in underpowered systems. Taking this into account, the following advice also reflects ways to reduce the amount of information rather than to suggest blind increases of resources.

- While it is known that the above-mentioned factors affect the reliability of IACS applications regularly, little monitoring is done. Monitoring is important wherever application behavior can change dynamically, such as in convergence scenarios.

Data Processing: CPU Processing Speed and Memory

It is well known that many IT systems in a control system environment operate near real-time. More than once, asset owners have experienced problems with critical applications due to insufficient processing speed or insufficient physical memory. For example, many asset owners have experienced problems when trying to install antivirus software on a SCADA server, DCS server, or operator's terminal for the simple reason of performance issues.

While it may be tempting to switch over to more powerful computers, chances are that this race cannot be won in the mid-term. Therefore, rather than increasing CPU performance and memory on the system in question, many operators have chosen to substitute for conventional antivirus using alternative solutions such as whitelisting, thereby freeing up both processing speed and memory.

Data Transport: Network Latency

A more delicate problem is related to network latency when accessing automation peripherals via the network. Latency may then exceed the tight timeouts that many industrial protocols use, and result in error situations that may be difficult for maintenance staff to analyze.

While the increased bandwidth of contemporary network gear has led many process network administrators to believe that worries about network performance are obsolete, this has proven illusionary. Network latency is not related directly to bandwidth. So, while bandwidth usually is no longer a problem, latency is. Depending on the number of network connections that a specific peripheral must handle and the number of hops (routers, gateways, switches on the way between source and destination), latency in the region of 1 second may build up. This may easily trigger error detection logic and cause the application to enter an error state.

> *A cluster of fully automated container cranes encountered frequent e-stops that were obviously triggered by internal system error states. Analysis revealed that the problem cause were timeouts in fail-safe communication that was done via the network—a highly cluttered network with much too high latencies.*

An alternative to installing more potent network gear is to disable network traffic that is not required in a specific segment of the process control network, such as voice-over-IP or other services that make heavy use of broadcast packets. Another strategy is to design process networks in such a way that network traffic between automation peripherals traverses as few routers and gateways as possible.

Data Storage: Disk Space and Access Speed

Data storage capacity may have two problems:

- There may be insufficient disk space, so that storage operations cannot be performed.
- Disk access operations may be too slow and result in the application being unable to process information within required performance limits.

While it may seem that nobody needs to worry about such problems today, since powerful disks are so cheap, data storage remains a problem for IACS environments. This may partly be due to the fact that DCS and SCADA applications create oceans of data that can quickly fill even the most potent database engine. It may also be due to the fact that, sometimes, much more information is stored than what is required.

> *During a review of backup procedures, it is determined that engineers perform a full disk image of a production system. This procedure was established simply because the engineers did not know which data and configuration files would be sufficient to restore the application.*

In situations where performance increases of the hardware used for data storage seem difficult, it is recommended to reduce the amount of information that is stored. Examples for this tactic include:

- Purging archive database files that contain outdated information
- Removing temporary files and outdated files, especially on shared folders
- Deleting outdated backups that are no longer needed on backup servers
- Deleting nonrequired applications and their associated disk files (see system hardening)

Robustification Procedure

Step 1. *Document what you have.* For the system under consideration and the performance characteristic under consideration, document the existing performance margin. To do this, select and use appropriate monitoring tools. The system integrator may help.

Step 2. *Document what you need.* For the system under consideration and the performance characteristic under consideration, document the performance margins actually required, based on projections and worst-case scenarios.

Step 3. *Identify and close the gaps.* Increase the performance margins of the system under consideration so that they meet requirements, or limit the load.

Step 4. *Document changes.* Document the new system configuration.

Step 5. *Pursue consistency and sustainability.* Make sure that any new identical or similar system uses the selected method of allocating performance reserves.

Chapter 8

Modifying Structure

Compared to cyberwar, change management is perhaps the least sexy subject one can imagine. Yet it is one of the most important subjects for control system reliability and maintainability. Many more problems have been caused in IACS environments by deliberate change than by dramatic, malicious cyber attacks.

Fragility observed: No organized and documented change management process exists; change comes by surprise and is handled ad-hoc.

Foundational requirement: Change is variation. If cyber changes are carried out in an organized and structured way, robustness is increased.

Robustness target: A binding formal documented procedure for change management as an ongoing process exists in the organization. A formal system for approving change is in place. Specifications for new systems and technologies are reviewed. The separation-of-duty principle is applied. Changes are tested in a lab environment before deployment. Changes are logged, properly documented, and reversible.

This chapter is brief because change management is very well understood in IT, and established procedures and standards such as ITIL can largely be adopted to control systems. It should also be noted that change management is nothing new to automation. It has been performed religiously for decades in the context of safety and certain regulated vertical industries such as pharmaceuticals.

8.1   The Need for Adaptability in IACS Environments

It may appear that the robustification principles outlined so far assume a static world. They seem to suggest that requirements are static and that system components, products and technology, vendors and contractors, procedures and configurations won't change over extended periods of time, and if replacement should be necessary, identical equipment will always be available. Even though many engineers try their best to keep IACS environments that way, they cannot succeed in the long term. Change is inevitable, even in static IACS environments with their long lifecycles. Progress is impossible without change. While the industrial cyber space is not nearly as dynamic as office IT, change does occur, though usually at longer intervals than in office IT. The need for and the principles of change management don't differ very much between the two fields. The challenge is not to prevent change, but to make sure that the system under consideration can be adapted to changed requirements with the least effort possible, without stumbling over existing cyber tripwires, and without installing new ones.

Since change is variation, the ability of a system to respond to change is directly related to its robustness or fragility. As illustrated by the "house of cards" example introduced in Chapter 1, a fragile system "breaks" during intentional, beneficial, and authorized attempts to modify its structure. The major difference between change and other sources of variation is that change rarely "just happens" (e.g., a malware outbreak or accidental misaddressing). Where change, or the need for change, comes as a surprise, poor planning usually becomes evident. For example, the need to migrate applications to upgraded execution environments such as new OS versions or advanced hardware interface technology can usually be anticipated years in advance.

Nevertheless, surprisingly few manufacturing organizations have implemented a formal change management process for IACS, even where ITIL processes are established and audited for office IT in the same organization. (Note: Indications are that the level of formal change management does show a relationship to industry. In manufacturing, change management is often rudimentary or nonexistent, whereas the process industries generally show more organized change.) A large number of cybertrips on the record can be attributed to sloppy change management, or no change management at all.

> *In an effort to keep operating system versions identical and current (for security reasons), IT staff in a paper processing plant update the operating system of a PC that is embedded in a paper cutting machine. After the update, the machine is dysfunctional, which cannot be explained by maintenance engineers (who were not even aware of the OS update), so the cutting machine vendor's technical support is involved. The vendor, after having done problem analysis, determines that the OS update causes the control system application to malfunction and reinstalls the obsolete OS version.*

Implementing change without proper planning and testing and not having process control tripped is proof of good luck. Improper or nonexisting change management often installs new cyber tripwires. Even worse, not updating system documentation after a change will soon result in getting back to the dark ages of insufficient system understanding, where engineering decisions are local, improvised, and based on intuition.

Robustification with no organized change management process cannot be sustainable. If no change management process is in place, robustification results will fade out gradually with inevitable change.

8.2   Change Factors

Compared to IT, IACS environments tend to be change-averse. There is little desire to check out new technology or products, sometimes in an intuitive understanding that changing a running system or just some system component might cause the system to crash. However, change cannot and should not be prevented. Here are some events and factors that drive change in the IACS space.

Flaw Remediation

The most trivial example of forced change is defect equipment that must be replaced, but no identical spare is available. More than one maintenance engineer in this situation has been caught by surprise. Since many IT and network products have a lifetime far shorter than typical IACS lifetimes, this scenario materializes frequently. If for any reason replacement is necessary, it may be impossible to procure an identical product (PC, operating system, network gear), because the specific vendor may be out of business or may have obsoleted the product or the technology (e.g., 10-Mbps hx network hubs). The only solution is to install a different product. In a fragile environment, this may result in far-reaching consequences.

> *A trained maintenance engineer replaced sensors in the substation of a power utility with nonidentical products, but forgot to update the SCADA system's configuration database. This led to erroneous values in the control room, to which an operator responded correctly. In an effort to solve the problem, the operator shortened a 145-kV transformer, which exploded and set the substation on fire. At that time, the maintenance engineer had already left the substation.*

Flaw remediation does not only apply to hardware. The following happens on an everyday basis: Operations detects a malfunction, and maintenance implements a bug fix (such as changes in ladder logic, configuration changes in network communications, etc.). The fix is not documented, and neither is it noted that similar plants may be affected as well.

> *After doing maintenance work on a specific machine, a contractor's maintenance engineer decides to install the latest software version on the machine's control system, just to get the machine in the best condition possible. Thereafter, the asset owner experiences problems with several other machines of the same type that happen to be network-connected to the machine that had undergone maintenance. Weeks later it was discovered that the problems were due to version conflicts between the machines with respect to the new software installed by the maintenance engineer.*

Optimization

Competitive organizations aim at optimizing their processes to maximize efficiency and reliability. Optimization, however, is change. Such change may affect day-to-day ladder logic enhancements in an effort to squeeze out the last percent of performance, or to cut away another half a percent of scrap. Unfortunately, unplanned, uncalled, and undocumented changes in ladder logic and similar process execution details have resulted in thousands of hours of downtime.

A contractor performs preventive maintenance on a machine at an automotive company. with the best intent, he installs the latest ladder logic version on the controllers. Thereafter, the machine works, but the asset owner notices that it doesn't perform as well as it used to. Weeks later, it is discovered that the contractor installed the new ladder logic, thereby overwriting many optimizations that the asset owner had applied over months.

Another and certainly noteworthy optimization effort is the application of robustification strategies as outlined in this book. As any optimization in design or process, they change the existing system. Such change may well lead to unwanted results if not integrated into an organized change management process.

Technological Progress

No matter how much some organizations or decision makers would like to stick to "proven" technology and products, at some point technological progress and falling prices will become convincing, and even the most conservative organization will take advantage of new products and technologies that offer better performance for the same or even a lower price. While IACS environments tend to be extremely conservative in adopting new technology, at some point even the biggest dam will break. For example, the introduction of TCP/IP and local area networks took place at a massive scale at the end of the 1990s, approximately 20 years after the technology itself became available in commercial IT products. This time lag gave many asset owners the confidence that the "new" technology was proven and reliable.

Advances in Infrastructure Technology, Design, and Architecture

With IT products being more and more adopted on the plant floor, asset owners can take advantage of performance improvements such as the following:

- Advances in computing hardware, such as going from single-core to multicore processors and hyperthreading
- Advances in network gear, such moving from network hubs to managed switches

- Advances in media technology, such as moving network cabling from copper to fiber optic, or introducing wireless LAN, RFID, USB, and SD memory cards
- Advances in design and architecture, such as server virtualization, VLAN technology, and remote VPN access
- The introduction of real-time Ethernet (such as Profibus, Ethercat, Ethernet/IP) as a replacement for conventional fieldbus technology
- Advances in IT architectures and interfaces, such as OPC UA and Web-based interfaces.

Innovative Applications and Functionality

Few IT-related environments are as static as plant floors. However, innovation does exist, even if the average timeframe for a new "killer" application is about a decade from invention to widespread use. So while dad's plant may have had little more complex cyber applications than SCADA or DCS, contemporary plants are usually equipped with two or three additional major cyber applications for enhanced productivity and competitiveness. Examples are

- Automated quality control
- OEE
- MES as a direct link between business processes and process control, allowing automatic downloading of recipe data, lot numbers, production quantities, scheduled and optimized by business logic, and uploading production progress, required resources, and amount of scrap (thereby allowing for calculating actual cost of production)

The introduction of such new applications usually is regarded as critical and may require several years.

Socioeconomical Factors

Besides technicalities, people and market realities may also drive change:

- Change in functional requirements may be mandated by policy, such as with a management decision to build new products, or to become compliant with regulation changes (examples: pharmaceuticals, nuclear).

- The buying decision for a migration or extension project, involving the purchase of SCADA, DCS, network, etc., products, may be in favor of a new vendor because of more attractive pricing or service offerings.

- An existing contractor or supplier may go out of business—not something very dramatic for product lifecycles of 20 years and longer.

- In a new geographic region where the organization has decided to establish a presence, products or services of a key supplier are not available, mandating use of a different source.

- Organizational fluctuation: Employees who leave or enter the organization, vendors and contractors whose contract is terminated or who are introduced to the organization, organizational changes such as department structure, outsourcing strategies etc.

With a cynical undertone, middle management of a company in the food and beverage industry complained that any new strategy effort for plant floor technology, products, and procedures would not be successful as long as the present management prevailed. There was, however, optimism that after present management retired, which was expected in the near future, company policy would change.

8.3   Change Management Quality Levels

Change management can be carried out at different, cumulative levels of quality. Cumulative means here that the tasks of a higher quality level don't substitute for those of a lower level, but enhance it.

Documentation

Criterion: Changes Are Documented

A prerequisite for any change management is an accurate and complete system model and documentation. The following sublevels of documentation accuracy can be found:

- Paper-and-pencil documentation
- Electronic documentation in Excel or Word (as local files on a maintenance engineer's computer system)

- Documentation in standardized format
- Documentation in a centralized database system

The general quality requirement for change documentation is that the documentation is comprehensible by people different from the change implementer, by the change implementer himself after a couple of years, and that the documentation can be verified to be accurate against the real system.

Testing

Criterion: Changes Are Tested Before Being Deployed in the Field:

For fragile systems, testing changes before rollout is essential, since it must be assumed that the system under consideration might misbehave after the change. This is one major reason why, among other things, automated deployment of operating system patches is prohibited in most installations. An operating system patch is a change of the execution environment that may cause alteration of system behavior—as too many asset owners have already experienced in real life.

Planning

Criterion: Changes Are Planned

Planned change requires the following formal documentation:

- A rationale for the change (requirement or benefits)
- A specification of the change
- A list of affected systems along with verification that the change does include all systems of a given category
- The identification of potential effects to associated systems, including version conflicts
- The timeline for the change
- The resources required (people, time, budget)

Unplanned change, or improvised change performed by heroic loners, may lead to disaster. Since potential side effects are sometimes very hard to predict, especially when an accurate system model does not exist, good planning without testing is of little value.

In some areas, such as safety-related changes or changes that affect high-value assets, planning may include a risk assessment.

Authorization

Criterion: Changes Are Authorized

For nontrivial change, planning might reveal that significant resources are required, or that side effects may be substantial. Therefore, it is a good idea to have some neutral person (i.e., someone not involved in the planning of the change) authorize the change. This is also called the separation-of-duty principle.

Reversibility

Criterion: Changes Are Reversible

In a perfect world, changes are reversible if it turns out that the change wasn't such a good idea after all. For some areas of change this is quite easy using commercially available technology, for other areas it's impossible. For example, software and configuration changes can usually be reversed within minutes where version control systems are used, while hardware changes that have been forced by a technology, product, or vendor that went out of market are almost irreversible.

Auditing

Criterion: The Change Management Process Is Audited

The change management process as detailed so far is a complex process. As a fact of life, complex processes that require the discipline, motivation, and education of humans tend to wear out. Therefore, any organization which puts emphasis on change management will audit the change management process every now and then. The goal here is not to put blame on people who missed part of their duty, but to make sure that the process is performed with a certain level of reliability even though few people take any satisfaction from it.

Epilogue

After reading through this book, the reader may have a feeling that he or she is planning, operating, or maintaining systems that are so complex they can no longer be understood in terms of all relevant cyber aspects and dependencies. For many complex industrial automation and control system networks, there is no longer any single person who fully understands the system, its subsystems, and their interactions, and neither is there accurate documentation that describes the system. There may be individuals, groups, or departments with a good understanding of parts of the system; however, experience shows that such groups—for example, networking and operations—don't communicate well with each other. Furthermore, these systems may be more complex than they have to be, and more fragile than should be tolerable. It is only a question of time as to when such systems will no longer be maintainable if they are allowed to continue to "grow" in the wild. "Growth" is random variation that occurs where the absence of planning leaves room for such.

One may still find an excuse to bury one's head in the sand—because the systems are not *defective* in a technical or legal sense, because there is no time budget to do anything about it, because it has always been this way, etc. Or one may decide that operating or maintaining a complex IACS installation that will soon (or does already) look like a complete mess of interconnected legacy systems and idiosyncratic procedures does not add to an engineer's job satisfaction. For the engineer who reaches such a conclusion, there is good news. One of the best aspects of the robustness concept is that it gives planners, developers, integrators, operators, and maintenance engineers an aiming point. Any new design, any change in procedure or technology, can be driven either in the direction of robustness or in the direction of fragility. No risk assessments or crystal balls are necessary. The move toward robustness can be started right here, right now. If this prospect seems appealing to enough engineers, the next evolutionary stage in control system design and operation might be characterized by a robustness leap.

Appendix

A   Surprise! Nonobvious, Nonanticipated Cyber Fragility Effects

Like many other complex systems, control networks show *nonlinear behavior*: Small causes may lead to big consequences. Change of cause and change of consequence do not necessarily have to be proportional. What makes things worse is that, in cyber space, cause and consequence may cross boundaries of function, time, and distance. They may appear to be completely unrelated. Therefore, some cyber-related problems are never analyzed, and many cyber-related problems will never show up in a fishbone cause-and-effect diagram (as used in quality engineering), because they appear to be completely nonintuitive.

One of the worst characteristics of cyber is that, unlike mechanics, there is no predictable degradation. In mechanics, problems usually build up gradually over time. Not so in cyber. Many cyber effects are not obvious and catch operators by surprise. The surprise may even exaggerate technical problems, especially when operators misinterpret system behavior based on the—inaccurate—model they have in mind. It then becomes obvious that the notion of having full control over a process was illusionary, even if the illusion worked for many years. Hidden, nonanticipated cyber effects that suddenly pop up and surprise operators and maintenance engineers challenge the operators' ability to operate the process reliably and safely. Surprise is proof of insufficient predictability.

Side Effects

Cyber side effects are effects on other, seemingly unrelated function groups *of the same system*. The affected function group is functionally unrelated

157

to the influencing function group and may well have been implemented by other people or other departments.

> *A real-time Ethernet RTU drops output signals when hit by a network scan on an unused port range; outputs are restored after the scan is completed. As there is no functional relationship between the IP driver and the signal driver (the relationship is functionally established only via a Profinet driver which uses a port range that is not accessed in this example), manipulation of output signal comes as a complete surprise.*
>
> *A SCADA application crashes when a memory and CPU power-consuming process (such as a virus scan) is executed on the same system. This behavior had not been anticipated because antivirus software has seemingly no relationship to the SCADA application.*
>
> *A label printer, barcode scanner, etc., fails, which causes a production halt. Due to the nature of logistics and business processes, the product cannot leave the present station without ID or ID scan and processing.*

"Quantum Leap" Effects

"Quantum leap" effects occur where incremental change in input parameters don't result in proportional change of output parameters but in a "leap" that is in essence similar to a qualitative change. This can usually be observed with analog parameters (see the model of cyber contingency layers discussed in the text), where variation beyond a certain limit makes the system under consideration enter another state, perhaps a nonfunctional state. Quantum leap effects can usually be explained by hidden thresholds (a.k.a. cyber tripwires). The thresholds are there from the beginning, but system designers, administrators, operators, and maintenance staff are not necessarily aware of them.

> *A protocol known as 3964R used to be popular for legacy field devices and controllers. The protocol was designed for RS-232 serial links. With the emergence of local area networks, many installations have been "upgraded" to network connectivity with simple RS-232/Ethernet gateways. As a result, asset owners experienced random loss of connectivity that could not be explained by laypeople. The reason used to be latency problems*

that occurred on the LAN side. As most people know, a latency of several seconds between packets is "normal" in Ethernet-based networks. 3964R, however, uses very tight timeouts (around 200 ms) to detect error situations. Such timeouts apply not only to acknowledgment messages, but also to intercharacter delays of data that makes up a data block (or "telegram"). Technically, it is therefore no surprise that this protocol cannot reliably be translated 1:1 to TCP. It comes as a surprise, though, to engineers who are not familiar with protocol details, either on the RS-232 or on the Ethernet side, especially since the resulting problems occur infrequently and randomly.

Cascade Effects

Cascade effects are effects *on other systems* and functions that are dependent on the disturbed unit or function of the system under consideration. As is well known, any distributed system is prone to cascade effects. For example, once a server process stumbles, clients will usually not be able to continue operations. A specific problem with IACS is that applications may be dependable on system services that don't have any user interface and perhaps even run in a different network segment, different subnet, etc.

Many asset owners have discovered that the failure of a domain server, NTP server, DHCP server, or network switch may cause other systems (such as DCS or SCADA server) to malfunction. Few commercial software products explicitly mention that such services are vital for undisturbed operation.

Ripple Effects

Cyber ripple effects propagate from one system through the network and affect multiple systems simultaneously.

In an automotive factory, network attached infrared scanners were used to scan product and material labels along the assembly line. Every now and then, all scanners failed simultaneously. Weeks later it was discovered that this was caused by broadcast packets that the scanners' network drivers simply could not handle.

Epidemic Effects

An overheat situation in one reactor, for example, will usually not spread to other reactors. A malware infection on one machine, on the other hand, may easily affect other machines, perhaps even *all* machines in a given installation/network. With epidemic effects, a problem is propagated from system to system throughout the network. The classic example is malware.

> *In 2005, the Zotob worm infected SCADA systems of what was then DaimlerChrysler. The worm propagated through the WAN connections of 13 interconnected plants in Illinois, Indiana, Wisconsin, Ohio, Delaware, and Michigan and caused a simultaneous production halt. Around 50,000 workers were put to rest during the system administrators' procedure for removing the worm, causing multimillion dollar damage.*
>
> *One of the most stunning aspects of the Stuxnet malware is that although in technical terms it doesn't spread like a conventional worm but like an old-style virus, it still infected thousands of systems outside its intended target area. So, even in a situation where distribution is intentionally limited to local infection, we have learned that local isn't local any longer—in a world where contractors have business with customers on multiple continents, where remote access is the norm, and where engineers are visiting multiple sites per week, every time carrying their notebook with them and attaching it to the customer's process network. Case in point: Hidden hubs are ubiquitous.*

Similar to ripple effects, epidemic effects are usually not prevented by redundancy.

Sleeper Effects

For sleeper effects, cause and consequence are separated by time. Problems may sleep for more than a decade until suddenly awakened by a change in the execution environment. Functionality that has been used flawlessly for years suddenly exhibits problems that have no obvious reason. Sleeper effects are usually related to sloppy change management, where they exhibit when system components (runtime environment, networking) are changed (updated, upgraded) with apparently no major change in function and alleged compatibility.

A paper mill is experiencing recurrent production halts due to a group of frozen PLCs. The networked PLCs have been in use for over a decade without any problems. Replacement of CPUs and network interfaces doesn't solve the problem. The PLC vendor is denying the possibility of any product problem, as the systems have performed flawlessly for many years. Problem analysis reveals that the problems started after upgrading the network switching gear from 10-Mbps to 10/100-Mbps auto-sensing. Subsequent analysis reveals that the old-style 10-Mbps half-duplex interfaces "react funny" to 100-Mbps auto-sensing packets of the switching gear.

A company in manufacturing had been operating a controller for a press successfully for many years. Eventually, the computer hardware needed to be upgraded. Everything else was to be left unchanged. After the upgrade, the press controller experienced random software crashes every other week. Two years after the system upgrade, the ultimate cause of the crashes was finally revealed: The computer was connected to the press controller via an RS-232 link with minimum wiring (2, 3, 7). Modem status lines (DCD, RI, CTS, DSR) had not been wired, leaving signals in random state. With the computer hardware that was used before the update, all signals had just been interpreted as a constant "zero" or "one." After the upgrade to new and much more sensitive interface hardware, modem status signals were interpreted as a wild switching between "zero" and "one," with up to several hundred status changes per second. This resulted in a driver freeze by overloading the driver with interrupts. Thus the original cause of the problem was not the computer upgrade but an inappropriately wired cable, which had been silently waiting to cause problems for years. Immediately after the cable was replaced, all problems were gone.

What can be observed here is known in philosophy as the "chicken problem," as introduced by philosopher Bertrand Russell. This problem is probably better known in its adaptation by Nassim Taleb in *The Black Swan* (Taleb, 2007). Taleb refers to it as the problem of the "Thanksgiving turkey." Viewed in the light of its experience, the turkey might establish the theory that it will be continue to be fed by its human keepers until the end of days. The day before Thanksgiving, however, will reveal that the turkey's theory is wrong; it will come as a surprise.

Remote Effects

Whereever remote access is possible, there is a chance for cyber-related problems that originate remotely. In this class of effects, cause and consequence are geographically separated. With the growing popularity of using wide-area networking for remote maintenance, remote effects where cause and consequence may be separated by many thousand miles are becoming more and more frequent.

> *A vendor is in charge of maintaining machinery for a customer in the automotive industry. The systems in question are installed at multiple sites around the globe. Maintenance is done through the asset owner's central dial-in point at headquarters in Germany. From there, traffic is routed through the asset owner's private WAN to the target system. While trying to connect to a target system in Canada, the maintenance engineer accidentally uses the target address of a similar system in the United States, which is stopped, reconfigured, and restarted in the process, causing five-digit dollar damage.*

Butterfly Effects

The original concept of the butterfly effect is rooted in the paradigm that a butterfly's wing may set off a tornado. The surprise factor here is due to the large disproportion between cause and consequence.

> *In 2006, a defective network attached controller at the Browns Ferry nuclear power plant in Alabama generated excessive traffic which caused the VFD controllers of both recirculation pumps to crash, and recirculation to stop. The operator decided to scram the plant manually in order to resolve the situation. "The reason the licensee at Browns Ferry investigated whether the failure of one device, the condensate demineralizer PLC, may have been a factor in causing the malfunction of the VFD controllers is that there is documentation of such failures in commercial process control. For instance, a memory malfunction of one device has been shown to cause a data storm by continually transmitting data that disrupts normal network operations resulting in other network devices becoming 'locked up' or nonresponsive. A network found to be operating outside of normal performance*

parameters with a device malfunctioning can affect devices on that network, the network as a whole, or interfacing components and systems. The effects could range from a slightly degraded performance to complete failure of the component or system. Major contributors to these network failures can be the addition of devices that are not compatible, network expansion without a procedure and an overall network plan in place, or the failure to maintain the operating environment for legacy devices already on the network" (NRC Information Notice 2007-15; Weiss, 2010) In the case of Browns Ferry, a fragile system design using 10-Mbps network hubs played a role in failure propagation.

B   Conservative Engineering Habits Resulting in Cyber Fragility

Robustness is not a new concept in engineering. For decades, engineers have learned to design and build robust systems—from the mechanical and electrical points of view. This is what is often referred to as "industrial-grade" design and implementation. Industrial grade is usually associated with long lifetime and heavy-duty operation, and with scenarios where the cost of breakage is substantially higher than the acquisition cost of equipment. Unfortunately, this culture did not extend to cyber. Why not? A closer look reveals that some traditional engineering philosophies may be counterproductive when applied to bits and bytes.

Discounting Cyber as a Nonessential, Virtual Add-on to "Real" (= Electrical, Mechanical) Functionality

Popular engineering culture has it that "real" engineering is hardware and mechanics. (A similar school of thought in IT argued long ago that "real" programmers would use C or assembly language.) Cyber capabilities of machinery are sometimes regarded as nice to have, but not essential. Associated with this thinking is the expectation that software and cyber functionality would not affect the price of components and machinery, at least not significantly. The purchase price for machinery can often be correlated to weight, and the same mindset assumes that software should not cost much because it can simply be copied.

Today, vendors have little ability to charge more by pointing out added cyber functionality. Thus, one should not expect that cyber robustness—which does not even increase the function set—would be a design goal for vendors, as it cannot be used to justify a higher price. Vendors must focus their development efforts on features that are critical for the buying decision. Cyber-robust products don't offer more functions, don't have higher performance, and don't necessarily have better economy than fragile products. Nowadays, with the emphasis on purchase price and feature set, a demand for cyber-robust products is not "natural." Robust devices usually increase reliability and maintainability, but these items only show in the long term, at some point when the person who made the buying decision may already have left the organization.

If a problem isn't obvious, one may fool oneself and others into believing that it doesn't exist. While a robust mechanical design often can be identified even by laypeople (a metal cover is used instead of plastic, thick wiring is used, etc.), cyber robustness is invisible in most of its aspects. Engineers and operators are just beginning to understand that bits, bytes, and software can have a similar or even more serious effect on system behavior than mechanical properties. However, even experienced engineers have little means to determine the cyber robustness of a given product. This has led to situations where it was assumed that there is no substantial difference between, for example, industrial-grade network switching gear and comparable products designed for home use. Certainly the cost is different. Therefore, many engineers opt for the low-cost solution even for industrial use, not understanding that the same quality differences may apply as with mechanical characteristics.

Overconfidence in Previous Success

Sometimes it appears that the ultimate goal of engineering is to make something "work" (either by design or by fix). If it then works, this is considered proof of success—*and proof of concept*. Sometimes engineering efforts stop at this point, without ever determining the circumstances under which the solution works, and those under which it won't. More than one engineer has been proud to get something to work just by trial and error, without ever understanding the system and its principles, and then putting the solution into operation. While trial and error may look empirical at first sight, the pitfall is that in the try-and-succeed situation (after which the system must not be "touched," see below), the reason for success is sometimes not really understood. Such poorly understood implementations may thereafter even become internal "de-facto standards," where later examination about the exact reasons for specific implementation details may be confronted with the killer argument, "Because it was always done this way." In ultimate consequence such reasoning may lead to some kind of superstitious engineering behavior where solutions are not selected based on experimental characteristics, but on "higher" principles of belief; with the associated assumption that following these higher principles will produce a working solution without actually knowing why.

Unfortunately, the fact that some solution, design, or implementation functions as intended is not proof of robustness as well. As long as the conditions for proper function are not specified and verified, the system in question cannot be robust, because malfunction may be imminent for unknown reasons. Fragile systems may function flawlessly for many years, but do so only as long as several undocumented (and perhaps unknown) parameters are met. A well-known proof for this principle is the financial crisis of 2008–2009, when financial risk management models and techniques failed miserably, even though they had been relied on for decades. Experience *seems* to prove stable functionality because it has never crashed—so far. The theory is that if a system has always worked in the past, it will continue to work in the future. What is seen here is the problem of predicting future behavior by inductive inference, which has already been discussed in reference to the philosophical problem of the Thanksgiving turkey along with the concept of naïve empiricism as discussed by Nassim Taleb (Taleb, 2007). With regard to robustness, history does not matter. A system may perform flawlessly for many years and yet be fragile.

> *The sophistication and aggressiveness of the Stuxnet malware was completely unprecedented in history. Nevertheless it materialized—and caught million asset owners by surprise. The fact that something like Stuxnet did not happen before had zero predictive value. Simply because such an attack did not happen, too many decision makers thought that it could not happen.*

Many engineers favor an intuitive approach to robustness which is expressed in the principle not to buy version 1.0 of any product. The accelerated version of this conservative approach is to buy products and technology only after they are considered "de-facto standard," i.e., used by a majority of peers with seemingly no major problems over a long period of time. Products and technologies are often avoided before they have "ripened" in other domains, other organizations, or other facilities. The average lag for adopting new control system technology is about 10 years, which is usually rationalized as follows: A new technology or product might exhibit flaws under different environmental conditions. If a technology, product, or vendor survives several years in many installations, this appears as proof of robustness.

While there seems to be some validity to this approach in that it might help to eliminate fragile products and technology just by evolution (extinction of fragility, survival of the fittest), the downside is that a successful product or technology (in market terms) is by no means necessarily robust. An example is OPC (OLE for process control), which is popular even though it came with serious fragility from day one. A large installation base alone does not prove robustness.

It can also be shown that many times, seemingly flawless installations do experience severe problems (e.g., with respect to network traffic) that are only visible when using appropriate monitoring methods. One day, for no particular reason, such problems may hit a cyber tripwire, causing process disruption. This will leave maintenance engineers wondering why a process suddenly fails after years of flawless operation (see the discussion of sleeper effects in Appendix A).

Heroic Engineering: Improvised Design Decisions and Configuration Changes ("Fixes") Leading to Systems That Must Not Be "Touched"

More often than most engineers would admit, cyber-related design decisions and problem "fixes" are improvised, or ad-hoc. The prime goal of ad-hoc design decisions is to make sure that the selected design "works"—under the circumstances given (which are rarely documented), and as quickly as possible. The engineer is expected to "fix it" *with the given tools and materials*, here and now, in the shortest time possible. If he does, he might be considered an expert, or even a genius or a hero who saved the day. This problem was solved only because of his or her individual expertise. Nobody else could have done it.

Even if one assumes that such hot fixes are well thought out and implemented by a genius, such practice will lead to inconsistent design and procedures if it does not follow a documented underlying design principle. Improvised design leads to variability in design, and cannot be verified against a design specification. It can also hardly be determined if an ad-hoc design decision meets all requirements. The generally accepted theory is that engineers, especially "real" engineers, don't have time to write documentation. This leads to the situation that many solutions aren't documented properly. Without proper documentation, a system is fragile per se, because robustness cannot be verified. Where a formal change management process for IACS installations is not in place, this may lead to changes that are not well planned, not in accordance with best practice, not properly documented, and perhaps not even properly tested.

This is the basis of the widespread engineering philosophy never to touch a running system (actually, the more proper phrasing should be, "Never touch a fragile system"), which can be understood as an intuitive way of the robustification principle of blocking invalid input. It may be discomforting, but one must conclude that this philosophy is an expression of incomplete understanding and mastery of technology: Systems must not be "touched" simply because it is expected that by just "touching" the system it will stop functioning properly. Systems that have not been "touched" for many years, as can be found frequently in real-life production environments, fail regularly and predictably when the environment changes. There are many situations where an individual process engineer has never "touched" certain equipment which may have been installed by a co-worker who has left the organization, usually without documenting the system properly. Such systems live on as little miracles. It is not understood why and how they work, and almost certainly it is not understood why and how they may fail.

Thinking Local and Present-Day

The flawed ad-hoc approach may also be motivated by the notion that some cyber application is just used to solve some little local problem—to get rid of a minor inconvenience, to provide some needed data a little better formatted, etc. Years later, the local workaround has become a de-facto standard. Living without that application seems impossible. As it turns out, it is no longer local (and never was), because it ties together different subprocesses or data flows just like a knot. Untangling that knot may prove difficult and expensive. End users may even view the flawed knot as a paradigm for how to design upgraded systems and demand a knotlike architecture during requirements engineering, no matter how weird it may appear to a neutral domain expert.

Any mid-size to large-size organization hosts examples of this: the small utility program that serves a very limited and very local purpose, developed by well-meaning employees or contractors. Often such a program closes a tiny gap that used to be conceived as a minor inconvenience, or provides a workaround for a glitch that nobody was able to explain causally. Because of its narrow scope, the utility program was implemented on the go by an employee in his spare time (because this fellow happened to play with Visual Basic for fun and recreation), or by a contractor for little money. It didn't look like the overhead of specification and documentation was worth it, so it was simply done without. Let's assume the small utility linked together two applications by means of using an FTP server here and a shared directory or database server there. Nothing essential, but now data can be passed from one application to another. Problem solved. That is... only assuming this specific environment, with very specific configuration settings for the applications that have been linked together. Due to time constraints and because it was just that little project, there is no proper documentation. Years later, the need arises to change the infrastructure and/or the linked applications or their configuration. Now it appears that the tiny utility has become an essential tool that operators cannot imagine living without; just by aging, it has become a de-facto standard. A severe case of lock-in is established, mostly because of bad (or nonexistent) planning.

Considering Only Best Case and Worst Case

If it has been argued in previous sections that in many control system designs, best-case conditions are assumed, that is certainly an exaggeration. Most engineers do consider failure. However, many restrict their scenarios to worst-case failures, such as network failure, while few include more common and more difficult situations such as increased network latency, broadcast storms, accidental misaddressing, etc. Fragility and robustness is not a binary decision; it is about navigating in a large gray zone that gets bigger with every added degree of freedom.

Abusing Flexibility for Quick-and-Dirty Implementation

Industrial Ethernet makes connectivity cheaper than preceding technologies and yet offers much more functionality. It becomes much easier to connect different systems; sometimes even so easy that connectivity is established without a compelling reason to do so. Such flexibility may be especially convenient during commissioning, when planning flaws or omissions surface. A workaround just out of the pocket may then save the day. Such workarounds never make it into documentation.

The reader is asked to carry out a thought experiment. Assume the era where point-to-point was the only connectivity option available. Now assume that even though dedicated cabling was required, establishing point-to-point connections was free; or, better yet, somebody would pay $5 for every additional point-to-point connection. Would it be worthwhile to inter-connect *all* systems? Probably not, because connecting systems that have no need to exchange data will only provide for potential failures, and because the resulting installation would look like a complete mess. Such systems are very hard to troubleshoot. In old-time point-to-point installations, the electrical engineer could simply identify a complex system by counting the plugs and wires that led to the attached peripherals. In a modern setup, there is only one connection—to the network. What seemingly is much less complex is in reality much more complex; the simplicity of industrial Ethernet is an optical illusion.

While in office IT, flexible network connectivity translates into more functions and services, the number of functions and services in process control networks is very limited and static. The ability to create ad-hoc connections between any systems with any port numbers may, however, be used to establish connectivity that simply had been forgotten in the design phase. Often this leads to spaghetti-like data flow patterns that are very hard to untangle and analyze. It also leads to large "open" networks with a high potential for malware spreads and increased chance of misaddressing (many similar systems that are only distinguishable by IP address or hostname, where hostnames provide for a high chance of ambiguity and errors).

Migrating Implementation Rather Than Function

Big-bang migrations are rarely seen in IACS environments. When confronted with inevitable change—for example, in the context of plant retrofits or when incorporating new technology—many engineers follow the philosophy of changing as little as possible, hoping that all the parts of the traditional design that aren't "touched" will continue to function flawlessly in the new context. However, changing as little as possible results in conserving design and implementation decisions that may not be appropriate for the new demands and features.

Such a "conservative" strategy can be seen, for example, where serial point-to-point protocols such as Modbus have been migrated to TCP/IP, where in many cases the data stream was sent over a TCP connection instead of the dedicated serial link. The philosophy to change as little as possible resulted in several design glitches, such as using tight polling loops on network links, using a stream-oriented protocol for packetized data, and not providing for authentication. Authentication was not a requirement (and therefore not a design feature) with old-style automation islands, where physical proximity was necessary to connect. With TCP/IP networks, it is essential.

Many migration and retrofit projects ended up consuming much more time and resources than anticipated by following the "change as little as possible" strategy, and more than one project leader determined in the aftermath that rebuilding the whole system in a big-bang approach would have been the better and more efficient choice. The underlying conceptual problem here is that function and implementation haven't been separated. Too often it is attempted to move implementation to another platform rather than implementing function in a way that fits the new platform best.

Being Shy to Confront Vendors and Contractors, the IT Department, and the Buying Department

This topic is mostly psychological but nevertheless real.

> *While there is a reasonable security culture in an organization (in terms of antivirus strategies, password change policy, operating system patch management, system access authorization, etc.), contractors are exempted by default from this culture. They may walk in with notebooks that aren't checked for patch level and antivirus software and have no restrictions on which network ports or systems to access. In the few instances where such contractors are questioned about this procedure in an effort to establish perimeter security, many of such contractors may be reluctant, "because we've known each other for 10 years and we've always done it this way". Surprisingly, most asset owners give in, thereby demonstrating that they trust contractors more than their own staff.*
>
> *A vendor refuses to implement robustness and/or security enhancements in his products or procedures, or only agrees to do so in return for ridiculously high compensation. The same vendor is highly dependent on the respective asset owner, which might be a global company and a major customer of the vendor. The customer accepts the vendor's behavior anyway, even though its buying department isn't shy in other regards, for example, squeezing the last fraction of a penny out of license fees per station.*

If a vendor or contractor doesn't perform in IT, the business relationship is usually terminated quickly. Not so in operations, where vendor and contractor loyalty is much higher. Products that lack capabilities or are full of bugs are accepted more frequently, sometimes even with the customer agreeing to pay for bug fixes. This is not about putting blame on contractors and vendors. It's simply about highlighting a rarely discussed subject that appears completely out of time and can only be explained psychologically, if at all. Similar observations can be made for intraorganizational conflicts.

> *Operations have determined that they need more robust automation and/or IT products and have redefined specifications accordingly. The effort is thwarted by the buying department because it would result in paying several dollars more per unit.*

C Cyber Robustness Versus IT Security

This whole book could be read as an attempt to put the control system cyber security approach as we know it, for example from ISA-99, into a bigger perspective; without the emphasis on malicious cyber attacks, and without speculations about potential attacks and attackers, their motivation, and capabilities. Ironically, the best reason for this is Stuxnet. The past 10 years of crystal-ball looking in control system cyber security did not prepare the world for Stuxnet-like attacks. And even after the fact, which demonstrated what few people deemed possible, asset owners see little need to prepare for the not-so-bright-looking future. One conclusion that can be drawn from these facts: Maybe it's time for a paradigm shift.

Cyber robustness and cyber security may be viewed as complementing paradigms, addressing similar, sometimes even identical problems. Many cyber security incidents may be attributed to cyber fragility, and increasing cyber robustness will reduce risk. This Appendix discusses the conceptual differences between robustness and security. In a nutshell, the fundamental difference is that the security approach teaches to *be careful,* where the robustness approach teaches to *be strong.*

Cyber Robustness Is Not About Information Security

It seems obvious for many to view industrial automation and control systems as just another type of IT equipment. That view is misleading, however. Control system security is usually viewed as a part of information security, with the major difference from office IT being that the priority of security objectives—confidentiality, integrity, and availability—are reversed to availability, integrity, and confidentiality. However, for control, the availability, integrity, and confidentiality of *information* are of little concern. Robustness and fragility are determined with respect to the reliability of executing a control function, whereas information security is concerned about the value that static information may present, and with potential ways to alter, steal, or delete such information. Information security has its roots in cryptography, where historically the paradigmatic problem was to protect military secrets that were broadcast by radio. The object to be protected is static in information security; it is information *content* that may ultimately be printed out. For control, there is no static object to be protected. The aim here is to reliably execute control logic within real time constraints.

While the term cyber in the IT domain refers to static information, in control it refers to behavior. One way to illustrate the difference is by imagining a cyber process as freezing. In IT, the corresponding (logical) process stops, resulting in a denial-of-service; in industrial automation, the physical process does not necessarily stop. A worse scenario is that the physical process continues with actuators frozen in unsafe conditions, resulting most likely in scrap and material damage.

The subject of control system robustness is a *control function* (sometimes also called *transfer function*), see Figure C-1, which spans three dimensions. Remember the function graphs shown earlier. These are actually simplified, as the third axis was omitted in order not to complicate matters. The third axis is time, or system state. The multidimensional characteristics of a control function cannot be adequately represented by the static concept of information as we find it in IT, and IT security in particular.

Language and terminology contributed to the confusion. In the context of cybernetics and automation, "cyber" is based on a different concept of information than what is used in IT. In cybernetics and automation, the term

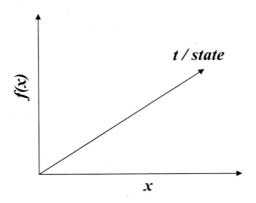

Figure C-1   A more accurate representation space for a control function: In addition to input and output values, it includes a third dimension for time or system state, which influence the behavior of complex control systems.

information does not refer to discrete messages, but to continuous conditions, which themselves relate to physical properties. Even though cyber also deals with information, or data, the concept of information is different from that in IT. In IACS, cyber is directly involved in the execution of the physical and/or chemical process that it governs. From a robustness perspective, it is therefore misleading to talk about *information integrity,* when a compromise of data integrity (recipes, for example) most directly and inevitably results in a manipulation of product properties, and therefore, in impaired quality.

- In information security (as in IT in general), information has *symbolic* reference to items in the real world, and to the damage that can result if the information is tampered with. Information and what the information refers to are completely different things, and the relationship between one and the other is totally arbitrary.

- In IACS environments and applications, data is *part of* a physical and/or chemical process. It does not make sense to isolate the data from the process, or vice versa, because the process doesn't exist without such data. Process data is a property of an automated process and affects every other process property, such as the efficiency of the process, or the quality of the resulting product.

For process control, the semiotic paradigm of information, as elaborated by philosophers such as Charles Sanders Pearce, is mostly inappropriate. This has large implications for the damage potential of disrupted or manipulated data, as in most cases, erroneous or malicious manipulations of process variables will result in immediate physical damage or monetary loss, whereas in the IT world, erroneous or malicious manipulations of data can often be corrected, thereby preventing damage, because there is only an abstract relation to the real world. In automation, there is no such thing as a "rollback" procedure, because it would require the ability to step back in time.

Cyber Robustness Is Not Related to Threats and Vulnerabilities

A threat is usually thought of as an extraordinary force or event that is outside of everyday operations, with the exception of military scenarios. In its root meaning, the term *threat* implies some form of aggression, or purposely and intentional harmful behavior of an opponent or hostile agent. ISA-99 defines threats as follows: "Threats describe possible actions that can be taken against a system" (ISA, 2007). In IT security, the discussion of threats is centered on attacks that may be attempted by nation states, cyber terrorists, saboteurs, spies, hackers, crackers, and malware authors. If there were no threats, there would be no need for security efforts. Vulnerabilities alone don't call for mitigation, because within the logical model of risk, a vulnerability is of concern not in itself but only in relation to threat. This is the basic rationale for risk assessment: If no threat can be identified, one may live with any number of vulnerabilities.

While any person in charge of a process control network who is afraid of performing a simple network scan, or who probably even knows positively that such a scan would result in damage, has any reason to fear cyber attackers, he or she is facing an even bigger problem. If trained staff acting in accordance with policy, as in the Hatch incident, is considered a "threat," this implies either stretching the concept of threat beyond reasonable limits, or the presence of a very fragile system—a system that doesn't require an attacker to be taken down. If typical procedures, and even planned changes in the operating environment, present a "threat" to a system, this is simply another way to say that the system is fragile. Such an installation does not have a security problem in the first place, but a problem with plant planning. Typical conditions *must* be included in the system's specification (requirements) and must therefore be reflected in system design and operational procedures. Where they are not, protection against untypical, perhaps even malicious conditions may be pointless and even absurd.

Fragility should be seen as a problem in itself. Robustification is rooted in the insight that it is impossible to predict events in the operating environment throughout the system's lifecycle with any reasonable accuracy, and that therefore fragility should be minimized even without being able to specify the potential cause of variation and change. Just by stochastics, fragility will sooner or later result in reliability and/or maintainability problems. Robustification teaches to aim at robust design and procedures every time, as it may not be possible to predict adverse conditions in the face of uncertainty with reasonable degree of success. This approach is aligned with modern software development standards, where the object-oriented approach is used not only for critical code sections, but as a design principle for every line of code.

IACS Vulnerabilities Are Different from IT Vulnerabilities

Even when following the threat/vulnerability concept, it is hard to ignore that vulnerabilities of industrial automation and control systems are quite different from vulnerabilities as they are known in office IT. Everybody who is using a desktop or notebook computer is familiar with security flaws, or vulnerabilities, that are fixed by applying a security "patch," which the vendor of the operating system or application makes available for free as soon as possible after learning about the vulnerability. Today, this process is largely automated, at least for the operating system, which has the built-in capability to download and install the latest security patches without user intervention (WSUS). Even though this capability of automated security patches is usually not activated on plant floor systems because more than one operator would not be amused if seeing a computer reboot and reconfigure automatically in a 24/7 environment, the capability as such is available.

On the other hand, most vulnerabilities related to industrial automation and control systems are not "bugs," or software defects, but "features," which have been designed into the product by purpose.

Vulnerabilities that are actually product features rather than bugs can't be fixed. Since they can't be fixed, they are here to stay. The author coined the term "iDay vulnerabilities" for this characteristic (as opposed to the much-discussed 0days, pronounced oh-days), expressing the fact that such vulnerabilities stay there for an infinite number of days, because they are not defects or oversights, but intentional product features. They won't go away, because "fixing" or "patching" such vulnerabilities would lead to version conflicts and incompatibilities that neither vendors nor asset owners would want.

Cyber Robustness Is Not About Defense and Attackers, or About External Factors in General

Security efforts aim at protecting against adversaries and their malicious activities by implementing proper countermeasures. The concepts of protection and countermeasure imply a hostile agent or action with the intent to damage the target system or target organization. The term *defense*, which is often used in the context of cyber security, assumes that there is an adversary against whom protection is called for and helpful. In accordance with the meaning of *threat* as discussed above, in common-sense thinking (and in terms of statistics), attacks by an adversary would be well outside everyday behavior. One may defend against hackers and spies, for example, but procedures to prevent equipment failure or accidental misconfiguration will hardly be called "defense." One does not "defend" against nature and entropy, against random events, or against users who accidentally do the wrong thing with the best intentions and compliant with policy. One does not "defend" against change (which would be outright foolish, as change will sooner or later confront the system anyway in order to meet the evolution of requirements). Robustification is not about defense and mitigation. It is not primarily *against* anything. The logic of the "against," which implicitly assumes some form of external antagonist, is out of scope for a robustness perspective. Robustification is not even "against" variation, since a static system is not adaptable to evolution of requirements.

If typical environmental occurrences (such as planned change) account for the majority of undesired output variation, the problem is not with the external factors but with system design. In terms of statistical process control, it could be said that as long as stochastic (common cause) factors account for the bulk of output variation, it doesn't make sense to search for an assignable cause or special cause (Deming, 1982) such as a cyber attack.

Look at the collapsed house of cards in Figure C-2. After building the house, the creator walked away and came back several hours later, to find the house collapsed. What caused it to collapse? Was it an attacker (such as the author's two-year-old son), was it a heavy truck driving by, or was it just a random gust of wind? Actually, this is the wrong question. Answering this question doesn't help much, because it could have been anything. If a specific cause may materialize just randomly, it isn't a specific cause anymore. It makes more sense to focus on the broken object's properties. For fragile systems, determining external (specific/assignable) cause of failure, or hypothesizing about potential external causes of failure is misleading, because potential causes for failure are all around in the typical environment of the target system and may occur just randomly. The ultimate cause of problems is not external; it is internal.

Imagine the house of cards being built outside on the porch. Theory and experience tell us that wind is a major "threat" to the house. One strategy, then, might be to shield the house with a big folding screen. Because the

Figure C-2 A collapsed fragile structure. Searching for external factors that might have caused the collapse, probably even for actors with malicious intent, is misleading.

screen looks messy on the porch, it is used only on windy days. Weather fore-casting is used to determine the periods when the screen is installed (early enough, and only as long as needed). Unfortunately, installing and removing the screen may itself cause the house of cards to collapse. (If parallels to con-temporary approaches in industrial cyber security are noticed, such as patch management, this is not an accident.) Getting back to IACS environments, if a fragile automation peripheral or control system fails or behaves "funny" when subjected to a ping sweep, network scan, OS security patch, antivirus signature update, etc., it might as well be misleading to explore (and protect against) the risk of a cyber attack.

Litmus Test: Does Robust Design Prevent Stuxnet-like Attacks?

After Stuxnet, any method and strategy that addresses control system secu-rity in one way or another must answer the question of how it would perform when confronted with a Stuxnet-like cyber attack.

Systems Protected by Conventional Wisdom and Policies

First, it must be stated that the traditional school of thought which applies prin-ciples of IT security to control systems fails to protect us against Stuxnet-like attacks, which is a major motivation for this book. To recap, what did *not* prevent Stuxnet and Stuxnet-like attacks?

- **Risk analysis:** Valid arguments that such attacks are technically pos-sible, and that they are even likely to happen, had little impact. The author had predicted a Stuxnet-like attack in early 2010, including target specifics (then identifying the Bushehr nuclear power plant as the most likely target). However, even after Stuxnet, and in the face of provable security vulnerabilities, asset owners in critical infrastructure and in the private sector didn't address the problem.

- **Patch management:** Timely installation of security patches doesn't help. While we don't know any details about the patch management policy in Natanz, we know one thing for sure: The latest security patches wouldn't have prevented Stuxnet from spreading, just because zero-day vulnerabilities had been exploited. One of these zero-day vul-nerabilities took the vendor (Microsoft) months to fix.

- **Antivirus solutions:** Antivirus software with current signatures doesn't help. It took antivirus companies about a year to incorporate signatures for Stuxnet in their products. We don't know when those signatures arrived on the systems installed in Natanz, but it can be speculated that there was an additional time lag.

- **Firewalls and defense-in-depth:** As far as we know, the systems in Natanz are isolated from the local network.

- **Authentication and encryption:** The infection process used by Stuxnet took advantage of a legitimate engineering station where an authorized user performs tasks with full administrator credentials. Stronger authentication or encrypted transmission between controller and engineering station would not have prevented Stuxnet from compromising controllers.

- **Air-gapping and physical access control:** If Stuxnet's target can be proud of anything, it's probably air-gapping and physical access control. There may be few places in the world, such as Fort Knox and Langley, where physical access is better controlled than in the Natanz fuel enrichment plant.

All the major items of standard control system security would not prevent Stuxnet.

Stuxnet Confronted with a Robust Environment

How would a robust installation respond to a Stuxnet-like attack? In short, it would survive such an attack easily. The chance of success would be near zero. In detail:

- There would have been little debate about whether such an attack is likely. Systems would have been robustified not in an effort to protect against specific potential attacks, but to increase overall system reliability.

- Policy and standard operating procedures would largely prohibit the use of thumb drives and would define strict rules for mobile engineering stations.

- IT systems, especially engineering stations, would be equipped with code execution and configuration tamper control such as application whitelisting. Therefore, malware would have little to zero chance for infecting such systems.

- General-purpose interfaces such as RPC would not exist.

- Stored SQL procedures would not be available.
- The ability to execute arbitrary code through application-specific interfaces would not exist.
- Shared folders would not exist.
- Hidden hubs would be eliminated.
- Different least-functionality interfaces would be used for SCADA and engineering access, thereby preventing the reconfiguration of controllers from SCADA systems.
- PLC manipulations would only be possible temporarily in situations that could be supervised closely by authorized staff.
- Ladder logic would be authenticated by digital signatures, thereby making code injections nearly impossible, or PLC configuration integrity monitoring would detect unauthorized PLC program changes early.
- Network exposure of engineering stations and PLCs would be restricted to authorized connections, thereby making access from and to other stations impossible.

Perhaps the most important aspect is that robust design and procedure would do all this without even speculating about the likelihood or potential damage of such malware, and without making any assumptions about the intentions of the forces behind such an attack.

This is not to say that robust design could withstand any, and especially even the most sophisticated cyber attacks designed and executed by cyber superpowers. It is just to state the plain fact that robust design would significantly reduce the chance for success for cyber attacks similar to Stuxnet to near zero.

D   Robustification Case Study

Project Pitch

A manufacturing company sets up a project to determine what alternatives exist to the regular application of operating system security patches for plant floor PCs. Several hundred systems are identified to enter into the project. All identified systems are hard or impossible to patch.

- *Impossible to patch* means that the operating system in use is out of the vendor's support window, and updating to a new operating system version is not possible because the application running on the system is not available for newer operating system versions. For some of applications in question, the vendor is no longer in business or has discontinued the product.

- *Hard to patch* means that significant amounts of money and labor would have to be invested because a hardware system upgrade would be required (the systems in question did not have the memory and CPU resources to run a newer operating system version) and the application update would cost major license fees, along with system reconfiguration and retraining of staff.

All applications in question worked flawlessly without the necessity to change anything, so the asset owner had good reason to attempt keeping them as they were.

The goal of the project was to modify the systems in a way that they could continue operation without posing a security threat to other systems, and with a risk of malware infections comparable to systems with current security patches. Since all systems in question were running static applications that had not been planned to be updated or changed for their remaining lifetimes, the only purpose for applying operating system patches was the prevention of malware infections. It was out of project scope to include any risk assessments with respect to malware, malicious insiders, etc. Therefore, no crystal-ball looking was necessary. The more detailed project goals were the following:

- The level of reliability and security after robustification should at least match the situation with continued security patches.
- The cost of the system changes should not be higher than that of continued security patches.
- Users should not experience notable drawbacks in functionality or additional workload.
- System changes should be kept to the minimum, especially with respect to installation of new software programs.

System Models and Documentation

At the time of project start, the exact number of systems to enter the project was unclear, and so was the question how the population of systems would be split into application groups. The asset owner once had implemented a

CMDB, but it turned out that the database had been outdated for several years and would be of no help. Information about affected systems that went into the project had to be gathered by interviewing maintenance staff.

As the project progressed, other system groups popped up, some running operating systems such as Windows NT 4.0 and Windows 98, which would officially not have been allowed to be connected to the asset owner's process network if policy had been followed.

Structural System Model

A system model of the applications running on the systems, along with interfaces and use cases, did not exist. Such models were created as part of the project by interviewing operators and maintenance engineers using questionnaires. In addition, sample systems were technically inspected, which resulted in some conflicts between mental system model and real system configuration. Technical inspection focused on obtaining a list of installed network services, security products, and transportable media.

Inspection of application functionality and data flow didn't show major problems or even high complexity. All application groups featured few simple relationships to other systems. For example, operator panels were talking to dedicated PLCs, and quality inspection systems to dedicated sensors.

Backups were performed mainly by copying data files to shared folders on a backup server. Several system groups accessed shared folders on a document server to supply maintenance staff with system documentation.

Getting Real

For each system group, data flow was verified with passive network scans. Scan results showed additional traffic that was largely unexpected for the asset owner. For example, Netbios connections from multiple stations was observed for some systems that could be explained by some obsolete procedures that were still configured. As anticipated, scan results for SMB showed traffic from many more systems than were specified.

Robustification Strategies

After analysis of the system models and specification, the following measures were selected:

- System hardening with the emphasis on disabling network services
- De-installation of antivirus software
- Installation of whitelisting software

After de-installing the antivirus software, several maintenance engineers experienced their systems performing considerably better than before. De-installation of AV was generally viewed as a step forward.

A small group of systems proved too complex to justify system hardening, and another group of systems was running Windows 98, for which no whitelisting solution was available. It was decided that these systems would be put into isolated quarantine networks; others were separated from the process control network by firewalls.

System Hardening

System inspection revealed that the usual network services (NetBIOS, DCOM, RPC, SMB, etc.) were running, without anybody having questioned why they might be needed. From an economics point of view, there is little reason to "patch" these services monthly when they are not needed for the applications that run on these systems. A deeper system inspection showed that most network services were not required, with the following exceptions:

- SMB was used to perform backups (to a shared folder residing on a central backup server).
- SMB was used to access engineering documents that were stored on a central document server.
- SMB was required for a SCADA application that used UNC path names.
- SMB was used for distributing configuration files among members of a specific application group.

The latter two exceptions were comparatively easy to solve. The systems with the SCADA application in question (which, by the way, also played a key role with Stuxnet) were reconfigured so that the SMB service was bound to the local host interface. Thereby, SMB was still running, allowing the use of UNC path names, but was no longer accessible via the network.

The configuration file distribution problem was solved by installing secure copy (SCP) on the affected systems. For the engineering documentation, it was determined that updates occurred only after several years, if ever during the client systems' lifetimes. It was also determined that the size of all documents that were required by maintenance engineers was small enough to fit on the local hard disks of the respective client systems. Therefore, it was decided to move documentation from the central document server to the local clients, eliminating the SMB connection.

Solving the Backup Problem

The backup problem wasn't as easy to solve. It soon became evident that the backup procedure using shared folders was a main issue in the project. There was little possibility of keeping the SMB service running on unpatched systems. An alternative needed to be found.

For one system group that didn't need network connectivity to run the application, it was contemplated that backups would simply be done locally to USB thumb drives. During discussion with the asset owner this suggestion was rejected because there was a record of stolen thumb drives even for internal USB interfaces that required the system chassis to be opened.

Since one stated project goal was to install as little software as possible on affected systems, it was determined that FTP would be an alternative to performing backups, since FTP clients are part of standard operating system installations for all OS versions in the project. However, some modification was required because standard FTP transmits authentication credentials unencrypted and thus lacks access control. To overcome this problem it was decided to pack backup files to password-protected ZIP archives on the client station and to use a modified FTP server software with the ability to check the archive's password automatically. The error handling/security procedure for the FTP server simply consists of (1) not accepting anything but ZIP archives and (2) checking the archive's password (archives that can't be opened are simply rejected, thereby dealing with potential DoS attacks and accidental FTP queries).

After several enhancements and add-ons to the FTP server software process, the asset owner was happy with the new backup procedure. An important aspect was the fact that operators experienced no difference in performing backups. The same backup scripts that had been in use for years were simply modified at the back end to use the new procedure and servers. Restore procedures were somewhat different because, for security reasons, the FTP server was implemented in a way that downloads were not possible, so the only way to restore a backup was to walk to the backup server, do a manual copy to a thumb drive, and install that copy on the respective client system. However, since this procedure was required only in the event of a system crash and was performed by maintenance engineers, the additional burden was accepted by the asset owner.

Cost/Benefit Analysis

Since the asset owner viewed this project as a pilot with the potential to be applied at a larger scale, a cost/benefit analysis was an important deliverable.

Cost of Patching

In many organizations, applying security patches has become some kind of religious exercise. Many people have stopped asking for a cost/benefit analysis. In a way, regular patching may even become evidence of fragility: When patches are applied with no good answer to the question of why it is necessary, it can be an indicator of inadequate system understanding. Many times, security patches and antivirus software are blind-shot measures advocated by people who have given up trying to understand their vital production systems—this despite the fact that operating system patches for control systems are notorious for problems. Patches cannot be applied automatically, and many asset owners had already run into problems with applications that behaved oddly after an OS patch was applied. Any operating system patch is a *change* of the execution environment, and there is no guarantee from Microsoft or other vendors that low-level functions of a control system application will perform flawlessly after the patch.

The cost of applying operating system patches is discounted in many organizations, since patches are available for free, and the application of patches is generally considered a necessity that doesn't need to be questioned. In this case, it turned out that (1) the asset owner did not have any realistic figure for the cost and (2) patching cost was much higher than had been assumed. The asset owner's patch policy involved the following stages:

1. IT filters patches for criticality and preapproves patches.
2. Local admins (= maintenance engineers) validate patches on test systems.

3. Local admins are free to reject patches if they feel the patch isn't necessary or will produce problems for the application in question.

The essential cost factors for patching are associated with manpower. Testing patches can be time-consuming, and it has to be done periodically for every patch. With an intuitive understanding of the labor involved, the asset owner had reduced patch cycles to once or twice per year. It was argued during the project that this resulted in way too low protection against malware. To make things worse, the exercised policy of good faith did not lead to auditable results. The level of protection achieved was not predictable. System inspection revealed different patch levels on nearly identical application groups.

Additional cost is associated with hardware and application software upgrades. For system lifecycles beyond 10 years, an asset owner is almost guaranteed to run into problems, because patches are usually only available for a time span of 10 years. Thereafter, an upgrade to a new operating system version becomes mandatory if patching is to be continued. Updating may, however, require the acquisition of more potent hardware, and application software versions that actually run on the new operating system.

Cost of Robustification

Robustification cost split mainly into the following areas:

- System analysis and documentation
- System hardening
- Procurement, installation, testing and rollout of whitelisting solution
- Development cost of the FTP backup solution
- For some application groups, firewalls to be procured, installed, and tested

It is easy to understand that the manpower required for system analysis, hardening, and testing is significant. Obviously, it is much easier to apply a security patch without determining whether the security flaw that is patched might belong to a network service or application that isn't needed anyway. The upside is that, for static systems as in this case, this effort is required only once, whereas patching is a recurring task throughout the system's lifetime. The good news is that the system hardening plus whitelisting approach is nearly service-free. Therefore, this approach is much more appealing than patching for systems that have a long lifetime and can be separated into large groups of nearly identical systems.

License fees for whitelisting software turned out to be unimportant, as the whitelisting software was used to replace the existing antivirus licenses, which could then be transferred to other systems.

Cost/Benefit Comparison

It turned out that the robustification approach required approximately one-tenth of the cost associated with following conventional IT security philosophy. For the benefit comparison, it was established that system robustness for the hardened systems was higher than for the patched systems.

References and Further Reading

References

Deming, William E. *Quality, Productivity, and Competitive Position.* MIT Press, Cambridge, MA, 1982.

International Society of Automation (ISA). *Security for Industrial Automation and Control Systems. Part 1: Terminology, Concepts, and Models,* ANSI/ISA-99.00.01-2007. ISA, Research Triangle Park, NC, 2007.

Kletz, Trevor. "What You Don't Have, Can't Leak." *Chemistry and Industry,* May 6, 1978, pp. 287–292.

Langner, Ralph, and Singer, Bryan L. "SCADA Threat Modeling Using Attack Scenarios." *Proceedings of the SCADA Security Scientific Symposium 2008.* Digital Bond Press, Sunrise, FL, 2008.

Shiller, Robert J. *The Subprime Solution: How Today's Global Financial Crisis Happened, and What To Do About It.* Princeton University Press, Princeton, NJ, 2008.

Sidi, Marcel. *Design of Robust Control Systems. From Classical to Modern Practical Approaches.* Krieger, Malabar, FL, 2001.

Singer, Bryan L. "Correlating Risk Events and Process Trends to Improve Reliability." *Proceedings of the SCADA Security Scientific Symposium 2010.* Digital Bond Press, Sunrise, FL, 2010.

Taleb, Nassim N. *The Black Swan. The Impact of the Highly Improbable.* Random House, New York, 2007.

Taguchi, Genichi, Chowdhury, Subir, and Wu, Yuin. *Taguchi's Quality Engineering Handbook.* Wiley, Hoboken, NJ, 2005.

United States Nuclear Regulatory Commission, Office of Nuclear Reactor Regulation, *NRC Information Notice 2007-15: Effects of Ethernet-Based, Non-Safety Related Controls on the Safe and Continued Operation of Nuclear Power Stations,* Washington, DC, April 17, 2007.

U.S.-Canada Power System Outage Task Force. *Final Report on the August 14, 2003 Blackout in the United States and Canada.* https://reports.energy.gov, April 2004.

Weiss, Joseph. *Protecting Industrial Control Systems from Electronic Threats.* Momentum, New York, 2010.

Wiener, Norbert. *Cybernetics, or Control and Communication in the Animal and the Machine,* 2nd ed. MIT Press, Cambridge, MA, 1965.

Further Reading

Shannon, Claude, and Weaver, Warren. *The Mathematical Theory of Communication.* University of Illinois Press, Urbana, 1949.

von Bertalanffy, Ludwig. *General Systems Theory. Foundations, Development, Applications,* 2nd ed. Braziller, New York, 1969.

List of Acronyms

ACL   Access control list. ACLs are a basic configuration option in firewalls and contemporary network switching gear that allows the filtering of traffic based on IP source/destination address and protocol.

AD   Active Directory. Proprietary network directory service for Microsoft Windows. Among other things, Active Directory can be used for central administration of user accounts and policy settings.

AV   Antivirus. A family of computer applications that try to prevent infection of computers with malware by comparing files that are going to be installed or stored on a computer system against a "blacklist" of known malware.

CAQ   Computer-assisted quality.

CIA   Confidentiality, integrity, and availability (of information). CIA is a central concept in IT security. It is not used in cyber robustness.

CIFS   Common Internet File System. IP-based network protocol and service for accessing files and folders on remote systems via the network.

CMDB   Configuration management database. A database that not only acts as a system inventory but also lists the specific configuration of systems, such as operating system version, patch level, etc.

COTS   Commercial off-the-shelf (as opposed to custom-built).

DCOM   Distributed Component Object Model. Proprietary technology for Microsoft Windows–based software that enables the use of software components across the local area network. DCOM has become infamous in automation environments because it comes with several security issues if it is not configured properly, but it is very difficult to configure.

DCS   Distributed control system. A control system that is composed of one or more IT systems and several controllers. The major difference to a SCADA system is that a process controlled by a DCS will discontinue to run without the IT part, whereas the IT part of a SCADA system is "only" for supervisory purposes.

DDE   Dynamic Data Exchange. Proprietary technology for Microsoft Windows–based software that allows for interapplication data sharing. In automation, DDE was used for accessing proprietary driver interfaces to automation peripherals in the days before DCOM was available. DDE drivers can still be found today in some installations.

DHCP   Dynamic Host Configuration Protocol. Auto-configuration client/server protocol for IP-based networks. Among other things, DHCP allows for automatic assignment of dynamic IP addresses to client computers.

DLL   Dynamic Link Library. Software library containing functions that may be linked to different Microsoft Windows applications at runtime, rather than at link time.

DNS   Domain Name System. DNS translates symbolic hostnames to IP address information.

DoS   Denial of service. DoS identifies a class of cyber attacks that aim at making the attacked system, service, or application unusable (at least temporarily). Examples of DoS attacks are ARP poisoning and the LAND attack. Most DoS attacks do not require insider knowledge.

ERP   Enterprise resource planning. ERP systems play a role in automation and control if they are connected to control systems, which is the idea behind manufacturing execution systems (MES).

FTP   File Transfer Protocol. Standardized IP-based protocol for transferring files via the network. Since FTP transmits user names and passwords unencrypted, it was replaced by more secure protocols such as SFTP in many installations.

GUI   Graphical user interface.

HMI   Human–machine interface. In a control system environment, HMIs can usually be found at operator terminals and SCADA/DCS client workstations. They are used to monitor and manipulate the process, for example, to change product recipes, to stop/resume production, or to inspect process alarms.

HVAC
Heating, ventilating, and air conditioning. HVAC may play a role in cyber robustification where a production process depends on it. Examples can be found in the food and beverage industry and when dealing with clean-room processes.

IACS
Industrial automation and control system. Even though ISA is moving toward the abbreviated acronym ICS (industrial control system), IACS is preferred here because automation peripherals without built-in intelligence and control logic are also prone to cyber fragility and should not be excluded from the system model for any robustification effort.

IO
Input/output, referring to the electrical signals of controllers.

IP
(1) International Protection rating, as defined in IEC 60529. IP protection classes are completely physical and have nothing to do with cyber. (2) Internet Protocol.

ISA
International Society of Automation (formerly Instrumentation, Systems, and Automation Society).

ISO
International Standards Organization. Among other things, ISO developed standards for data communication which became known under the name OSI.

ITIL
Information Technology Infrastructure Library. ITIL is basically a standardized set of best practices with a major focus on IT service management.

IRC
Internet Relay Chat. Protocol and service for real-time text message exchange via the Internet. Among other things, IRC has become infamous for being used by malware to establish stealth communications with a command-and-control server.

JRE
Java Runtime Environment. Applications written in the Java programming language are executed in an interpreter-like runtime environment, including a "virtual machine." In the past, JREs caused trouble due to version conflicts.

MES
Manufacturing execution system. An MES links business processes, mainly order processing, with automated production processes. This may include pushing lot information such as quantity and recipe information downstream to controls systems. Plant floor systems, on the other hand, push information about production process and product quality upstream to the business process.

MoM | Message-oriented middleware. Software that allows applications from different vendors to interchange discrete free-form messages. Message-oriented middleware is often used by enterprise software applications to exchange data.

MTTR | Mean time to recover. The average time it takes for a system or service to resume operation after system fault or disruption, based on empirical observation.

NFS | Network File System. Protocol and service originally developed by Sun Microsystems to access disk storage via the network. NFS is still popular in Unix and Linux environments.

NTP | Network Time Protocol. A standardized protocol for synchronizing system clocks via the network.

OEE | Overall equipment efficiency. OEE is a key performance indicator for expressing the efficiency of a specific resource, such as a machine or an assembly line. OEE is computed by multiplying asset availability, performance, and quality of output.

OPC | OLE for Process Control. Standardized component software interface that is popular for accessing automation peripherals from Microsoft Windows applications.

OS | Operating system.

OSHA | U.S. Occupational Safety and Health Administration.

OSI | Open Systems Interconnection. Standardized protocol framework and suite developed by ISO for system- and vendor-independent data communications. While the protocols defined by OSI were made more or less obsolete by TCP/IP, the OSI seven-layer model of data communications is still in widespread use, even though it doesn't match well with IP-based protocols.

PCN | Process control network.

PLC | Programmable logic controller.

QoS | Quality of service. QoS refers to certain characteristics of network transmission, such as bandwidth, error rate, and latency. Some applications, such as voice-over-IP and automation protocols, have tight QoS requirements.

RADIUS | Remote Authentication Dial-In User Service. Network protocol and service that is used to automatically authenticate dial-in users and other nonpermanent network clients.

RAID | Redundant array of independent disks.

RFC	Request for comments. The standards that determine how Internet-related protocols and procedures are implemented are called requests for comments for historical reasons. Every standard Internet protocol and procedure, such as TCP or HTTP, is documented in an RFC that can be looked up via the Internet.
RFID	Radio-frequency identification.
RPC	Remote Procedure Call. Standardized IP-based protocol for interprocess communication.
RTU	Remote terminal unit. RTUs are used to connect decentralized electrical I/O points to controllers. While traditionally RTUs used point-to-point and fieldbus protocols for data transfer, most contemporary products are network-connected.
SCADA	Supervisory control and data acquisition.
SCP	Secure Copy. Network protocol for securely transferring data files from one system to another. SCP supports encryption and authentication based on digital certificates.
SFTP	Secure File Transfer Protocol. Standardized IP-based protocol for transferring files via the network and manipulating remote files. Different from old-style plain FTP, SFTP uses encrypted channels and provides for secure authentication.
SIS	Safety instrumented systems.
SLA	Service-level agreement. A SLA is an essential part of contracted (IT) services, in which the guaranteed delivery time or performance is specified.
SMB	Server Message Block. A protocol used in the Microsoft Windows operating system for file and directory sharing.
SNMP	Simple Network Management Protocol.
SOAP	Simple Object Access Protocol.
SOP	Standard operating procedure.
SPC	Statistical process control. In quality engineering, SPC is used to determine and enhance the predictability of a specific system or process to deliver product within specification limits.
SUC	System under consideration.
TPM	Total Productive Maintenance. A school of thought in manufacturing that aims at optimizing automated production processes by minimizing loss, which is expressed as either loss in availability,

loss in performance, or loss in quality. In TPM, Pareto charts play a significant role in identifying the major loss factors for a given operation. A Pareto chart is simply a sorted frequency graph in which the frequency distribution is from highest to lowest, thereby allowing for easy determination of the biggest (and thus most relevant) loss factors.

UML   Unified Modeling Language. A general modeling language that is used mostly in software engineering but can be applied in other fields as well.

VFD   Variable-frequency drive. A drive with adjustable speed.

VLAN   Virtual Local-Area Network. VLAN is a standardized network technology that allows one to segment networks on the Ethernet level.

VNC   Virtual network computing. Remote desktop control software for duplicating screen content, keyboard input, and mouse movements via the network.

VPN   Virtual private network.

WAN   Wide area network.

WLAN   Wireless local area network.

WSUS   Windows Server Update Service. Software update service for automatically updating Microsoft software products.

XML   Extensible Markup Language. Text-based data description language that can be used to represent arbitrary data structures.

Y2K   Year 2000.

Index